BILLIONS
BLUNDERS
AND
BALONEY

BILLIONS
BLUNDERS
AND
BALONEY

THE FANTASTIC STORY OF HOW UNCLE SAM

IS SQUANDERING YOUR MONEY OVERSEAS

Eugene W. Castle

ILLUSTRATED

THE DEVIN-ADAIR COMPANY • NEW YORK

1955

Canadian agents: Thomas Nelson & Sons, Toronto
Library of Congress Catalogue Card No. 55–6355
Printed in the United States of America

PREFACE

Why are Americans so unpopular abroad?

Why do our so-called Allies, after accepting our billions, resent us personally? Why do those whom we've aided insult us?

What brought about this unhappy relationship? How can we change it?

As a veteran of World War I and an active propagandist for Uncle Sam in World War II, I am vastly concerned with finding the answers to these questions. As a private citizen seeking no special favors and without Government pay or official status, I have become distressingly aware, after 30 crossings of the oceans and traveling the entire globe—Australia and the Iron Curtain excepted—that such resentment, bordering on open hostility, *does* exist worldwide *and it is increasing*.

In my 75,000 miles of foreign travel over the past three years, I have diligently sought to find out why; why we have failed so miserably in Europe and in Asia.

The answer, it has seemed to me, cannot be had in the itineraries taken by our Congressmen, Senators and other high officials to places throughout the globe where welcomes are ostentatiously staged and hosts are on dress parade. So I have avoided these beaten highways.

The answers, I have felt, must come from the peoples themselves. And these I have interviewed, as well as some of their leaders and the men who help mold their thinking. The shopkeeper, the traveling merchant, the housewife, the factory manager, the industrial worker, the banker, the publisher, the editor, the reporter, the surgeon, the concierge in the hotel, the waiter in the restaurant—these, as well as officials of foreign governments and the man in the street, are among the thousands with whom I have talked.

From them I have learned that the canvas is clouded with the blunders, wrong guesses, bad timing and gross extravagances of well-meaning but pathetically unqualified American policy makers and representatives.

To me it is an appalling story, most of which, I am sure, is unknown to the American people.

The story should be told, so that people may know what they're buying with their billions; so that the colossal errors of Yesterday and Today may not be repeated Tomorrow. It is in this spirit that I present my narrative.

Eugene W. Castle

CONTENTS

BILLIONS
BLUNDERS
AND
BALONEY

1

One American's Tour—A Personal Narrative

It was in the land of the Pharaohs that the vivid contrast between Russian propaganda and our own hit me squarely between the eyes.

I had just left the serene and ritzy Nile River international section of Cairo, the ultrarespectable district of affluence and smug content where the United States Information Agency, our official global propaganda organization, has its principal headquarters for Egypt. My companion and I had marveled at the lush décor of the USIA buildings, the expensive furnishings, the air of gentility and the abundant staffing.

"You Americans," my Egyptian companion said, "surely have tools here to do the job. Your Uncle Sam, he has given everything, and with a lavish hand."

It was quite a distance, he observed with a quizzical glance, between our propaganda headquarters and the busy native sections of the city.

"Just what is the job, Mr. Castle, that you Americans are trying to do here?" he asked.

I told him of the assignment given the United States Information Agency (henceforth USIA) by our Government. "Briefly, it is to create and foster goodwill for America; to counteract Soviet Big Lies with the truth and to induce you and the other free peoples of the world to feel as friendly toward us as we feel toward you."

"Those sound like noble objectives," he commented warmly; "and just how does your USIA go about it?"

As we made our way toward busy downtown Cairo, I tried to tell him. "USIA's field of operations is the whole wide world. The methods and devices it employs have been left almost wholly to its own determination. It is what we call back in the States an independent office of our Government."

"Your President or maybe your Prime Minister, is he its boss?"

"USIA is pretty much its own boss," I replied. "Its work is supervised very lightly. Its ideas are pretty much its own."

"Ah," he replied, "I see."

As we approached the heart of downtown Cairo I suddenly became overpoweringly conscious of the Russian way of propaganda.

A Soviet trade delegation arrived one fine day and announced it would spend considerable time in Egypt looking into the heavy machinery and industrial equipment requirements of Egypt's projected plunge into progress. Fat King Farouk had lost his throne, and the Egyptians were in a stern and purposeful mood.

Moscow had it timed right on the button.

The Russians had spent six months investigating and $150,000 promoting an industrial exhibition. It was set up in the center of Cairo, in such a well-chosen place that sooner or later every Egyptian there was bound to see it as I saw it now.

The Reds made special plans to induce the masses to come to the exhibit. Inside the structure were all kinds, sorts and sizes of machinery, powerful and efficient looking, every piece marked "made in the USSR." The barefooted, ragged Arab masses who trooped in and wandered around, wide-eyed and open-mouthed, didn't know what they were looking at or what it was all about, but it was something to see and talk about in the bazaars and native quarters, a change in their dull lives. And while they understood nothing whatsoever of the uses for the machines and equipment, they were impressed with the size and magnificence and overpowering quality of the exhibit.

So was Cairo's youth, whom the Reds treated with particular consideration. Students—young people just feeling their oats and, by their very natures at this time in their lives, seething with rebellion against everything and everybody "old-fashioned"—are always helpful to the Communists, who have spent much time studying them in every country in order to figure out short cuts to win them over to the Red side.

After the "made in the USSR" exhibit had served its purpose, the premises were closed briefly. When they were re-opened, with much fanfare, there was a new show. The wily Comrades had switched all the pieces around on the floor so that the appearance of the exhibit was entirely changed, and the machines now all bore shiny new nameplates stamped "made in East Germany."

After everybody had viewed this great demonstration of the wonders accomplished in that part of Germany under the beneficent supervision and administration of the German Communists' Russian mentors, the show closed down once more for a couple of weeks. When it was re-opened, the same machines had been moved to still other positions on the floor, and now were wearing nameplates proclaiming Czecho-Slovakia as their point of origin.

This three-in-one exhibit which was seen by millions, applauded over and over by the native press, was an excellent example of really effective Red-style propaganda. Then, early in 1954, the Russians raised their ministry in Cairo to an embassy, thus directly courting and flattering the new Egyptian government; and, as a final touch, an important trade deal, ostensibly barter, was negotiated between Egypt and Moscow.

The Comrades really know how to get maximum mileage out of an idea.

I talked to a couple of intelligent Egyptian businessmen about all this. One of them represents an American automobile firm, the other a famous American product.

"What do we Americans do to counteract this Russian propaganda?" I asked them.

They both shrugged. For a moment they were thoughtful and seemed disinclined to speak. I pressed the point: "What about our propaganda here?"

"You really want the truth?" the younger one asked.

"Nothing but," I answered.

He shrugged again.

"Well," he said, "your American propaganda establishment is completely out of bounds. Egyptian soldiers guard the property day and night. The American setup is in a fashionable residential section . . . poor Egyptians would never go out there. Individually, they wouldn't have any business there so they wouldn't waste time going just to look at the buildings.

If a group of them went out, or even a small crowd, they'd probably get excited and chatter—our people are quite excitable. And the soldiers would chase them away. They're not looking for trouble and excitable crowds here always spell trouble. So what good does it do your country to have this big establishment in the foreign section of the city?"

"That is so," the second man chimed in. "Your propaganda establishments suit the convenience of the well-dressed people who man them. I think they are not seriously interested in changing the thinking of the Arab world to make them understand and like America and American ways. They are more interested, I think, in living a luxurious, easy life here and sending fine reports back to Washington."

I sought confirmation or denial of this viewpoint from the Amid brothers, Ali and Maiskapa, who publish and edit the important Arab newspaper, *Akh Bak El Youm.* They subscribe to the Associated Press wire service and to the Reuter's, the British press service, as well as to the Egyptian News Agency, the leading Arabic news-gathering service.

The two brothers are big men, physically; worldly

men, well educated, and thoroughly familiar with
America and its institutions since they both were grad-
uated from George Washington University.

"Do you get any of our material from USIA?" I asked
them.

"Yes, it comes over from your Embassy every day."

"What do you do with it? Do you use it?"

They looked at each other and at me and smiled.

"Oh, once in a while," Ali said. "The only time we're
interested in the American propaganda is when the releases contain an important speech by an important
American official and it isn't fully reported by the AP
or Reuter's or our own service. You know that we are
newspapermen, getting out a paper in Cairo for Mos-
lems. We must choose our news accordingly. So, 70%
of what we run is news of the Moslem world; 20%,
about, is European news; and 10%, sometimes 12%, is
American news. That is our idea of the proper proportion of interest. With the three wire services our
coverage is complete—we don't need to resort to a propaganda sheet.

"We don't need or want propaganda of any sort
from any government," they explained further. "We've
been exposed to it for years. We can tell it a long distance away. The very fact that it has a government
label on it stamps it as propaganda—instantly. Before
we even open the envelopes, we know what's inside."

"So, then, you feel this is a useless service—this wire-
less material sent from Washington to the USIA in
Cairo and delivered to you and the other newspapers?"
I asked.

"We do," they said flatly and firmly. "We are not

propagandists for any government—except an occasional important speech."

This was the answer I had received before in other countries. I was to hear it from reputable men to whom I put the question in every country I visited.

I wasn't through with the Amids, however.

"How about the Voice of America?" I asked. "Does that do any good?"

"It comes in very early in the morning. Nobody listens to it here."

"What about the slick pamphlets and magazines?"

"Those are sent out by the USIA to a selected list of persons—liberals and intelligentsia. Believe me," said one of the brothers, "these people have no influence on Egyptian life—the people on the list. And even *they* take no stock in these fancy publications of your government."

I was determined to get to the very end of this.

"Well, do we have *anything* at all that goes here?" I asked. "For instance, what about the mobile units—the movie trucks? Any of them operating around Egypt?"

"No," they both exclaimed at once, with considerable feeling. "We couldn't permit that kind of thing —movies with loud-speakers in congested villages, or even in congested sections of the city. Our people are very excitable, you know. We just couldn't have it. Anything might happen."

"Are you against all American propaganda movies?"

"No, not at all. There are lots of good educational pictures we like. But they're shown by the American-supported colleges here and in other cities in the Moslem countries."

"So we don't need a big 6-story, air-conditioned building for all this USIA activity then?"

"Well, if you want to spend your money no one here will stop you. We believe your government's reliable postage would be better to bring some of this printed matter direct to individuals here. People could feel they were being specially chosen for the direct compliment of a package or an envelope full of interesting mail from America, direct."

That was it. I took my leave shortly after, thanking the editors and wondering why we persist in behaving everywhere abroad like Al Capp's kigmies, for every last one of our government-sponsored information projects appears to make every American a kigmy—a little animal that just likes to be kicked around.

In Turkey and Greece the story with variations was the same. What makes our situation really ridiculous, pathetically so, in both countries, is that there is no legitimate reason whatsoever for any USIA activities in either of these countries. The Turks have fought the Russians 17 times in 40 years, and they'll keep on fighting them. The Turk is not the kind of man who'll take any guff from anyone, least of all from a Communist.

Istanbul is a fine place for roaming. It's a beautiful city, full of history and drama, and it's the finest example of real progress and assimilation of constructive western ideas in the Middle East or anywhere else for that matter. Many European cities with inflated ideas of their cultural importance and contempt for anything outside their own borders could take a leaf from Turkey's book.

There are 12 or 15 newspapers in Istanbul and I

struck up a fine friendship with a local reporter. He took me on a tour of the city, showing me with great and pardonable pride its most famed landmark— St. Sophia Mosque, once a Christian church, then a mosque, now a national museum, with its priceless treasures, including the matchless Christian mosaics so prized by the Turkish government it has had experts cleaning and repairing them for the past 25 years. We went through the bazaars, especially the big one with its 92 separate streets, each with small stalls selling a separate line of goods. It is here that some of the finest jewels in the world change hands.

One day after a fine dinner at Abdullah's, a 75-year-old restaurant that is one of the finest in Europe, I said I'd like to meet and talk with the editor of the leading paper. My friend agreed to take me to his office the following day.

When we arrived we were neither spoken to nor greeted in any way. We just sat down in chairs and I watched this apparently eccentric man with fascinated amazement for about 15 minutes. He was short and squat, with a crew cut, a rather odd choice of haircut for a man in his late 50's or early 60's, I thought. He sat at a desk in a room which had three doors, through which a continuous stream of men flowed in and out. One would come forward and thrust a piece of copy paper into the editor's hand. He'd read it quickly, mark it or not, as he saw fit, and hand it back without a word, and the fellow would leave just as silently. Or he'd read the copy and wad it into a ball, throw it into the wastebasket and dismiss the unlucky one with a wave of his hand. I finally got bored watching this silent performance and asked my guide how much longer he thought we'd have to wait.

Just then, the editor turned around and spoke in Turkish to my friend. What he asked, I learned afterwards, was simply, "What does this man want?"

I composed a little speech in which I said I recognized Turkey as one of the really dependable allies America had—one of the few—and that I'd like his opinion on our million-dollar-a-year propaganda program to promote Americanism in Turkey and maintain good relations with his country.

He spoke crisply and to the point—and, to my surprise, in English.

"There are no 'Yanks Go Home' signs in Turkey," he said. "Turks like Yanks; Yanks like Turks. The only Yanks Turks don't like are your propagandists all over our country. If *they* would go home it would be still better for Turkish-American relations."

With that he stood up, advanced toward us, shook hands with the reporter and with me, bowed and sat down. We left.

Seldom had so much meaning been conveyed in so few words and so little time—and to so few listeners. It was such a meaty summing up of the whole story, not just in Turkey but everywhere, that I think this incident, more than anything else on this trip, sold me on the idea of putting the show on the road, so to speak; of telling Americans at home what this one American on tour, a kind of reporter-at-large poking around, asking questions, had found out for himself and the rest of us.

It was in Greece, though, that an able, highly regarded and influential Greek editor put the topper on the Turkish comment. He told me the Greeks had learned that American propaganda excesses and explosive statements from high Washington spokesmen have created the belief among the Soviet policy makers that all Americans live in constant fear of them. This is exactly the condition the Communists strive to bring about, he said. We are helping them, he added, by what in Greece is believed to be Washington's 'round-the-clock irritation of Moscow. He thought the situation was further complicated to our detriment because while American spokesmen talk about peace and tranquility—and, he added, we Greeks know they mean it—they also continually talk *for* the aims and objectives of Soviet propaganda and infiltration through this odd American propaganda.

In other words, by spending several millions of dollars for United States Government propaganda in Turkey and Greece alone we are only creating the impression with the people of these two countries, he repeated, that we are terrified of the Communists.

Our talk went on for some time, and I learned, further, that informed and intelligent Greeks deplore the totally mistaken notion of Washington that all foreign peoples spend most of their time thinking about the American brand of democracy and ideals which the paid American propagandists are continually broadcasting everywhere in the world.

"The truth is, that even those who are most grateful for what Americans have done for them just don't want to have this dinned into their ears day in and day out. This overdose of American propaganda is like the man who said he loved steak and so his best friend gave him thick steaks three times a day, every day of the week. No normal man could fail to get tired of this diet and would even begin to object forcibly to it after a while," the editor said. "The same thing is true of ordinary people and your propaganda.

"We are your friends," he said. "We don't need your propaganda. Tell your government that. We subscribe to the American news services. They tell us a better story of America and what it's all about than these press releases from amateurs."

When I left this fine Greek citizen's office in the ancient city of Athens, I wandered downtown to meet several Greek businessmen who represent American companies. I'd known a couple of them a long time, done business with them, understood them, just as they understood me. We spoke man to man, not as American and Greek.

One of them, the one I'd known longest, shook his head sadly when I told him about my talk with the editor.

"Greece is a country of old relics and old men," he said. "Sometimes the old *human* relics speak great truths. Did you know that within the past few months 40,000 of our youngest men have migrated to Australia? They can't make a living in Greece. We are everlastingly grateful to America for saving our country from the Reds. We Greeks love America. But we are poor, and I must confess that it is a source of some irritation to us to see you throwing away money as you do.

"We can't understand why you have to spend millions of dollars a year selling America to Greeks. We like you! You don't have to try to buy something you've already got. We wish you'd figure out some other way to use your money to our mutual advantage; some way, perhaps, that would keep our youth here, not send them so far from their homeland to make a living in an alien country and an alien culture."

Then I traveled to Rome. I was enjoying an excellent Italian luncheon one afternoon in a good restaurant— what restaurant in Rome isn't good? The hour was late and the crowd had thinned out. Presently the proprietor whom I had known from previous visits came over and spoke to me. Soon he was seated beside me, at my invitation, and we were off on my *favorite* topic—how were we doing in Italy with our American propaganda? The *restaurateur,* like so many Roman businessmen, was an extremely cultivated and knowledgeable fellow. He had perception and wit and since he had come in contact with a lot of Americans—tourists and residents—he had some solid opinions on American-Italian relations.

"When new people come from the States to join your government's big establishments here in Rome," he said, "they first seem to want to mingle with the local people to learn our language, how we live, how we think, what we like and don't like; to discover what kind of people we are, in essence. This intense interest, I've noticed, usually lasts only three weeks or a month at best, with most of your people. After that they seem to abandon the idea of becoming part of the community, even of learning the language for their own profit and pleasure. They live apart then—apart from Italians, that is—and go about only with individuals or groups from the thousands of other Americans in government service here in Rome and throughout Italy. I have watched this for years now. It is too bad that these Americans who come here representing the American Government cannot get closer to the average Italian. If they did, they might understand us better and we surely would understand them better.

"This is all very sad to me when I think of the inroads the Communists have made among our working people. Americans have done nothing to counteract this. What I mean by this is that all the American money and efforts have not succeeded in counteracting this Red activity here. So we must seek for the reason why. Money, propaganda, fine buildings in the best streets will not, of themselves, make for better American-Italian relations to offset Communism."

He paused a moment to fill my glass and to tell me a little about the wine. "It is the wine of Verona," he said. "From Romeo and Juliet's city. A very romantic wine." Then he went on.

"I think one of the chief reasons why American aid and your propaganda have both failed here is that you say you are doing these things to fight Communism in Italy. Italians don't understand why Americans in Italy should know more about this than Italians. You always seem to overlook the fact that the Russians do not staff their propaganda offices here with Russians. They operate with misguided Italians who influence other Italians —millions of them, unfortunately. These Italian Communists, not the Russian Communists, teach and preach hatred of Americans. If you could only think in terms of understanding the Italian people, especially the poorer working classes—that would help. Your people here who are paid to do that just don't.

"A few years ago when the Communists were making a strong effort to take over the Italian government—as they are still trying to do—they never stop trying—thousands of letters that poured in here from Italians in the United States to their relatives in Italy defeated the Communist effort that year. This letter-writing, this personal testimony of the worth of America and American ideas from Italians living there, or Italians who had become Americans, did more to sell America and Americans to Italy than all your billions spent for aid and propaganda. And it was much cheaper for Americans. Everybody just bought letter paper and stamps, for a few cents. It was wonderful, and so effective." He shook his head.

"Excuse me, signor, I must go now," he said rising suddenly and shaking my hand. He left hurriedly. He had become emotional, thinking and talking about the errors which were so plain to see and which, uncorrected, are bound to create such havoc. It gave me a bit of a start, too, to hear this further confirmation of a story that was tragic in its repetition all the way from Cairo, through the Near East, to Rome. I had no doubts that France would just be more of the same.

And it was. But since the French are realists, with such cold political cynicism that it is a chilling experience for any American to be exposed to it long, I determined to look for a little wit to leaven the bitter conversational fare I knew would be served me.

I got both. The big, hearty senior editor of a Parisian newspaper as well known and important in France as the New York *Times* or the Chicago *Tribune* in the United States, accepted my invitation to lunch.

"*Mon ami,*" he said, "what do you want me to say about your USIS?" (Foreigners still call the agency by its former State Department alphabetical designation.)

"I can raise your blood pressure or I can lower it. I can raise it by saying your USIS is useful. That is what so many Americans want passionately to hear. Or I can put your blood pressure down by telling you your USIS is useless. Which do you want?" he asked me with that cynicism I have come to associate so completely with the French intellectual.

"Just tell me the truth in your own words," I said. "I can take it."

"*Bon!*" he said. "Here we go then. To commence . . . Here is what I, a French editor, have to put up with. On Monday, on page one, we have *M. le Président,* your Mr. Eisenhower. On Tuesday, on page one, we have your Secretary *d'état,* Mr. Dulles. On Wednesday, on page one, we have your Senator from the *fromage* state. On Thursday, on the front page, we again have Mr. Eisenhower. On Friday, that is *poisson* day in France, we have Mr. Dulles *encore.* On Saturday, on page one, we have the Senator from the *fromage* state again.

"Thank God we do not publish on Sunday."

I kept still, quite a feat for me in any circumstances, a matter of real will power in these.

"This is trivial, you think? But it is serious, I tell you," the editor said. "I do not speak like this to make the joke. I tell you the truth as we French see it. Americans are shallow. They are not as old as Europe and they do not think things through. I have been in your country and I know the Americans. You are a very young, vigorous people. Did you ever stop to think what those big healthy people in your middle west, in Kansas say, the people we see with a big hamburger in one hand and a glass of malted milk in the other hand . . . did you ever stop to think what those good people would think if the faces of French politicians appeared on the front pages of their newspapers day after day, all the time?

"Sometimes it seems to us who are editing papers here in France that all politicians, the top ones, the cabinet, the assistant cabinet, the 96 senators and most of the representatives want to be on the front pages of foreign papers all over the world. This is not good for America."

The editor leaned back and patted his expansive, expensive belly and if I had a momentary resentment I put it away because I knew he was giving me the solid truth, paying me the tribute of believing I was an honest man who wanted facts, who would not resent honest criticism. He was not buttering me up, giving me a lot of lies he thought I'd like to hear.

We understood each other; and while it irked me to hear this criticism of my country's policies from a foreigner, I had to admit to myself we had invited it and were doing nothing to dilute it or change it. Actually, we were rubbing salt in wounds that had never healed and, what is worse, we were doing it like ignorant, interfering morons, hopped up with a lot of political evangelism, hell-bent on being world savers and reformers, like a lot of busybodies fighting off their inferiority complexes with destructive little hand-out hatchets.

My luncheon companion sensed my mood and he said, "Let me illustrate what I mean about your propaganda by telling you a story. I have a Belgian friend, a lively fellow even though he is a bit elderly now, and he comes to Paris every so often to see the girls."

I interrupted him at this point to inquire what was the matter with the Belgian girls.

"Oh they are all right," the Frenchman said, "but our French girls here in Paris, they are better. So one day my Belgian friend and I are walking along the Boulevard and we were talking together about all these buildings you Americans have here, bulging with propagandists . . . people I am sure who would have difficulty working for legitimate newspapers," he added with utter frankness.

"My friend from Belgium said wouldn't it be wonderful if all the propagandists for America and all the propagandists for the Soviets would take a long holiday. If that could be arranged, he said, there'd be a lot more happiness in the world."

It galled me to hear Americans and Russians put in the same category like this but I was there for information, not to start a fight, so I took a long drink and the Frenchman accepted another from the second bottle of wine that made its appearance as if by magic.

"You see, the Russians do not employ propagandists. At the Russian Embassy there is only a press attaché and some books. If you go there you'll be lucky if you find the attaché in and who wants to read their books? Even if you could get at them! The Russians use local comrades, French Communists. The Communist Party in France does all the work for Moscow and, what is more, Moscow makes the French branch of the party pay all the bills for Communist propaganda here." He began to laugh heartily. "What a joke! These French Communists do not call themselves Communists. They are 'Nationalists.' And the Russians take a free ride on this local group. They do it in all the countries where the natives are fools enough to let them," he added.

"Well," I asked impatiently, "how do we compete with that?"

"You could do it very easily, *mon ami*, and far more cheaply than you are trying to do it now. France has so many political parties it is made to order for the simple way you could take. You could just hire some press agents, shall we say, some good Frenchmen in each of the political parties. You wouldn't have to pay them too much. Then every time someone writes a nasty letter to the papers about Americans, your paid press agent could answer *toute de suite*.

"*Voila!* It is as simple as that. And it would be effective. These French press agents of yours would do far better for you than your own corps of paid propagandists. They do not answer any insults to America now, to say nothing of just plain nasty letters. Why does your embassy let the movie about the Americans dropping the atom bomb on Hiroshima during the last war run on indefinitely at the theater here in Paris? Nobody has said a word of protest. Your propagandists say nothing, do nothing."

I was to remember this comment about the Communists' propaganda use of this film when I saw an item about it in *Variety*, the theatrical weekly. On Wednesday, April 14, 1954, *Variety* stated:

"Propaganda-conscious Americans returning from Paris report a Japanese-made film, 'Les Infants d' Hiroshima,' has been showing for months at Le Vendôme, a cinema on Avenue de l'Opéra in the heart of the French capital. This film is but plenty against the U. S. A. in its implications.

"Why, ask the returning Americans, has the U. S. Embassy in Paris apparently never protested this long run when a Parisian ordinance limits American films to five weeks in any one theater?"

Then there was the elderly government civil service employee who told me, "Perhaps there are too many American government workers in Paris, and they only serve to remind the Frenchmen of their own overstaffed government. There is this difference, however, and it does not help good relations. French government workers are paid like paupers and have to live like paupers; American government workers here are paid and live like kings. That makes for jealousy and bad will—the Communist agitators feed on it."

He lapsed then into a philosophic mood. "Never forget that the average Frenchman is always an individualist. We admire enthusiastic, outspoken people. It is the French character to look with suspicion upon all who preach to them or tell them how they should live. I think we French liked you Americans best when you told us your sanitary facilities were much better than ours. This was back in the mad twenties. Then Frenchmen used to exclaim: 'What wonderful people! What comfort they enjoy! We French must someday have better toilets, like our rich American friends.' Your tales about your toilets were the best propaganda for the Frenchman—and it cost you nothing."

A successful French commercial agent, M. Allane, whom I have known personally and favorably for many years, said this to me in Paris in late March, 1954:

"In reality, Communism in France is an economic disease. It is the same in Italy. Communism flourishes where there is wild inflation and unemployment. Inflation results in the workers' salaries going continually downward in relation to their purchases of the necessities of life. Americans have given billions to France to speed up the economic recovery of French industries whose operations were retarded during the war. Americans are spending upwards of $4 million annually to propagandize the French people.

"In Paris alone your propagandists occupy elaborate chateaus and establishments located in the center of the gardens of the Champs Élysées. Additionally, throughout both France and Italy you maintain extensive propaganda and cultural establishments. These efforts have not succeeded in arresting the growth of Communism in France. During the past year the Communist Party of Italy has added a quarter of a million members. Your expensive efforts have had little if any success.

"Why is this so? What can you do? Let me cite the situation in France. Italy is much the same. In Italy over-population is an additional factor that works for Moscow."

As to France:

"If your Government had rehabilitated the earning power of even a fraction of the industrial workers of France and Italy at the same time that your billions rehabilitated the industrialists of these countries then the local Communists would boast of fewer converts to

Communism today and probably by many millions. It would have been relatively easy for Americans to accomplish this.

"When you ladled out the vast sums of money you could have done so on the firm condition that, at regular intervals agreed upon in advance, the French industrialists receiving these funds would agree to raise the salaries of their workers in proportion to the benefits that they, the industrialists, received from America.

"Thus, instead of giving away billions of dollars to bolster the properties of the French industrialists, who, like most people of means, think of themselves first unless they are brought face to face with their larger obligations—if you had firmly insisted that the first beneficiaries of your aid dollars could not receive these dollars without spending some of them on their own workers, if you had done this from the start in France and in Italy you would have had the masses of the people, the workers of these countries, applauding the Americans who *raised* their salaries.

"Under such happy circumstances the Communist agitators would have had little if any success because they would have been unable to chant that American billions are making the wealthy French industrialists richer and the French workers poorer.

"Remember, Communism feeds on the empty market basket and dinner pail. Your 10 millions for propaganda each year in France and Italy do not fill these baskets or pails. It is as simple and as unappetizing as that."

After a lengthy pause, the French commercial agent continued:

"If you must spend money for propaganda it would

be much cheaper and more productive for your Government to invite a few managers and workers, mostly the latter, to come to America and observe for themselves the operation of American industries; also the high standards of living and the luxuries enjoyed by the great majority of America's working people. Propaganda films and other devices created by the United States Government will not convey this situation even if they present an accurate portrayal of your industries and the workers' living conditions.

"Remember, these people are unbelievers. They are of a desperate and depressed mind, otherwise they would not be Communists. Therefore, they must actually see to be convinced. If a relatively small number see for themselves they will tell others and you will have a real underground for Americans—something that you do not have today. Take for example, 50 employees from each of the following important French industrial plants: Renault, Citroen, Michelin Tires, also 50 ore miners and 50 coal miners.

"Let these people travel in the United States for two weeks by themselves. Let them go where they please and without any pressure or assistance. If they could be accompanied by their wives, so much the better. This may all sound impractical but a few hundred French workers and a few hundred Italian workers could do more to sell America to Frenchmen and Italians than all of the propagandists.

"Do something like this, plus telling the French and the Italians that all of their industries, luxury hotels, restaurants, silks, wines, cravats, women's clothing, tourist revenues—everything that brings contact with

the outside world and trade and revenue from the world
—would be locked behind an iron curtain forever if the
Communists gained control.

"Such efforts as these would in quick time enable you
to lock up the chateaus and other high-priced real estate in the heart of Paris and elsewhere that is today
wholly populated by the press agents of your Government. Then you could turn these buildings back to the
French and automatically stop homegrown Communist
agitators in their never-ending criticism of the great extravagance of the American propaganda machine and
their wild assurances to French men and women that all
this is to enable the capitalists to capture the world, or
something equally untrue. France is a country of middle
class people—it is safest and strongest when the middle
class are happy—they are individualists and to win
them no gusher of propaganda will ever replace reason
and logic."

And then I went down to Nice. Out in the countryside
one day, I encountered a surgeon. He was on his way to
perform an operation on an elderly French farmer and I
went along with him, accompanying him to the hospital
and waiting with him while he scrubbed up. We talked
all the time of world affairs, and about our separate
countries and especially about American propaganda
efforts in the south of France. Just before he went into
the operating room he said to me, "The trouble with
Americans is that you believe that a show of extravagance backed by your dollars will buy anything anywhere in the world. That is not so—this sick man I am
about to operate on needs my services and he can buy

them but he cannot buy my mind, or even my friendship.
Your Washington officials do not understand this simple
fact of life. If they did there might be less Communism in
France today."

In Nice, too, I saw on the walls of the city, all over that
lovely Riviera resort, shocking posters condemning
America for putting the Rosenberg traitors to death.
The posters were all the same—a big, blown-up head of
President Eisenhower, with a wide grin, showing all his
teeth; and set in every one of the grossly oversized teeth
in this caricature was a little electric chair. The legend
on the poster was: "Eisenhower! Assassin!" The posters
were often framed by brazenly misleading handbills
shouting: "Save the Rosenbergs!", and reciting dozens
of downright lies about these American traitors who
stole atom secrets and passed them on to Russia and
were tried and convicted and finally executed after one
of the longest series of appeals on record in the United
States.

Obviously these posters had been pasted on the walls
during the world-wide Communist campaign to stir up
hatred of America by distorting the facts. The campaign reached its pitch in the spring and early summer
of 1953. In the winter following, the posters, tattered
and torn by wind and rain and weather, were still on
the walls of Nice, and not a single municipal, provincial
or national official in Nice had lifted a finger against
them, nor had a single American voice protested. Not a
line appeared in the papers in our own country until an
American columnist published the story in late spring
1954.

By the time I was ready to leave Europe I had come to

the conclusion that future American researchers and scholars who sit down to write the history of their government's operations in the second half of this century will need four eyes apiece and two sets of indestructible ears per man to get through the tons of paper and miles of film and radio tape recordings in the archives. Some of it will be solid fact and strong testimony; much of it will be bibble-babble and gibble-gabble, the mush-mouthed maunderings of misguided men and their retinues of human parakeets, the self-serving propagandists who made profitable careers out of inept propaganda.

Our fighting men won the toughest war in America's history, World War II. They pitched in and took on a bloody "police action" in Korea. They had that war won, too, when they were stopped short of victory.

All this time there was another army forming, the battalions of USIA's mimeograph machines and typewriters, and the FOA's Handout Squadrons, enlisted in the Battles of GAB and GIVE.

That's the war we've *really* lost.

Such was Europe's reaction to our propaganda and our give-aways, as I found it. I went back to America to take the measure and make searching analysis of both.

2

Billions, Blunders and Baloney

Back in America, what did I find?

I found the incredible. Consider, for a moment, our official propaganda only. I ask you:

Do you know that the American taxpayer has paid out more than $400,000,000 since 1948 for foreign propaganda *alone?*

Do you know that for this tidy sum we have bought ourselves, instead of friendship, a hundredfold increase of anti-Americanism 'round the globe?

And that this is only a very small item in our giant catalogue of misspent *billions,* world-wide *blunders* and incredible *baloney?*

These findings, which are proved, confront the American people challengingly as they face solemn foreign policy decisions.

An astute American diplomat recently gave impressive testimony to this unpleasant truth.

Joseph P. Kennedy, former U. S. Ambassador to Great Britain and presently a member of the (Hoover) Commission on Organization of the Executive Branch of the Government, after an extended visit abroad, had this to say:

"There is something wrong with our propaganda. We spent 30 billion dollars in post-war Europe, but the man in the street there sees little evidence of it.

"Our propaganda is weak in Europe because the Russian propaganda appeals to the economic problems of the workers while we speak of liberty, freedom and democracy.

"A great many persons there think we, rather than the Russians, are the war party. That means Russian propaganda has been much more successful than ours."

For almost a decade the United States has been engaged in a stupendous campaign to win world friendship.

We have bestowed military and economic aid upon 43 nations, not including those in this hemisphere.

We have entered 22 top level international bodies and agencies, each of which has involved us in wider and more costly overseas obligations and commitments.

In disregard of our own national interests, we have exported American resources, techniques and know-how while baring our home market to the world, including those whose aim is to destroy us. We have underwritten UNRRA, UN and ECA and NATO and MSA and FOA.* And to reassure our Allies and to safeguard our-

* Respectively, United Nations Relief and Rehabilitation Administration; United Nations; Economic Cooperation Administration; North Atlantic Treaty Organization; Mutual Security Administration, and Foreign Operations Administration.

selves we have sent manpower after money by stationing
six Army divisions in Europe and by building and manning airfields throughout the world.

It has been a giant-scale, year-after-year give-away
program with woefully inadequate conditions, restric-
tions and safeguards; a program unmatched by any nation since history began!

We gambled our tens of billions of dollars in the confident expectation—and on our politicians' promises and
predictions—that overseas unfriendliness would evapo-
rate. But unfortunately the reverse has been the result.
We have given away our patrimony, but foreign trouble-
spots have multiplied against us. The relations with our
alleged friends and supposed Allies abroad have actually
worsened. Today, the plain American citizen who has
had an opportunity to observe our standing in foreign
lands must conclude that we have reached an all-time
low in global goodwill.

The truly disheartening thing about this situation is
that our national policy makers frankly declare that
more give-aways and more hit-or-miss foreign propaganda is their primary program for the years that lie
ahead.

President Eisenhower, in his otherwise admirable
speech before the 1954 annual convention of the American Legion, gave a conspicuously important place to
"propaganda" in the steps which he urged against Communist aggression. The significant point in his discussion was his statement that Soviet Russia is now spending
fifty dollars on propaganda to our one. The inference is
plain that a stepping up of our propaganda expenditures
in some such ratio is under contemplation. The Presi-

dent placed this emphasis despite the fact that nine years of American post-war propaganda, not backed by strong national policies, have utterly failed to win for the United States the respect of foreign peoples.

Shortly after the President spoke from Washington, NATO Chief Alfred M. Gruenther, while visiting the United States, bemoaned the ineffectiveness of American propaganda overseas and acknowledged the impact of Soviet efforts in this field. Unfortunately, General Gruenther failed to mention that the successes of Russian propaganda invariably have paralleled Russian accomplishments in the field of world diplomacy. Also, it is perhaps a tragic circumstance that the Headquarters of the United Nations affords the Soviet spokesmen a world podium for their double talk and phony peace offensives, all lavishly press-agented under the dateline "New York, U. S. A." Thus, the Russians project their chief foreign policy spokesmen and their constant abuse of the United States to the entire world and from *within* the United States!

A trigger event that revealed the basic unhealthiness of our foreign relations was our utter rout at the Geneva Conference.

Understandably, Secretary John Foster Dulles went to Europe on the eve of Geneva strong in the conviction that America could count on its Allies to back its play against the Communist axis. Particularly, he counted upon Great Britain and France. Each of these countries was under a staggering weight of obligation to us. Since July 1, 1940, Britain had received from the United States in grants, loans and Lend-Lease the unbelievable

sum of $36,670,220,000; and the carry-over World War
I debt was $5,606,005,000. France had received in the
same period $7,707,000,000. Mr. Dulles speedily found,
to his dismay, that this generosity on the part of the
American people had been travel on a one-way street.

Anticipating Communist traps, Mr. Dulles tried to
safeguard the Conference by committing the United
States, Britain and France to an advance program of
joint action. The British and the French promptly
spurned both the idea and the program. Mr. Dulles
thereupon endeavored to commit Britain to joint Anglo-
American aid to France and Indo-China if needed.

Prime Minister Churchill quickly rejected this proposal. The French next proceeded to give the death blow
to the European Defense Community (EDC) which was
the cornerstone of all America's defense policies in Europe. The effect of Franco-British refusal to follow the
American lead was to leave us naked in the face of Communism at a supreme crisis of the Cold War. It was a
frightening demonstration of the abject failure of our
multi-billion-dollar "Sell America" effort since 1945. It
revealed, for all to see, our stark friendlessness in the
contemporary world.

When a major national program collapses so miserably, our search for the causes should begin with ourselves. Obviously, there must be something basically and
terribly wrong with a policy which can lead us to such a
juncture. One that has taken us from a big mess to a
still bigger one! Somehow, somewhere, America has
taken the wrong road in its endeavor to make itself respected and liked.

3

We Gave Them Billions

The most alarming thing in the present American situation is our growing isolation in the world. Today, as never before, the United States stands alone.

The immediate American problem is not alone the 800,000,000 Soviet-inspired captives behind the Iron Curtain who are being indoctrinated, from the cradle up, with anti-American emotion, We also face a Free World which is drawing steadily away from us. Dislike, even hatred of Americans, is endemic among our so-called Allies. Let us glance briefly at a few random instances:

In Chateauroux, France, 156 miles south of Paris, is located one of America's great air bases. For three years, a great concentration of American airmen and mechanics has centered on this field. They have lived side by side with the French people in this community.

Not long ago, disturbed by some unfriendly episodes, the Air Force conducted a poll of the Chateauroux residents on their attitude toward Americans. The results were appalling.

Only 10 per cent of the Frenchmen sampled professed friendship for the Americans; 57 per cent expressed various shades of dislike and declared they wanted no association with the air base personnel. The balance had no opinion.

The sting of this is that Chateauroux is one of the bases which the United States maintains at great expense to secure France from possible attack from the east. We protect them, but they detest us.

In Britain, open unfriendliness toward American objectives is becoming so thick you can cut it with a knife. The action of ex-Prime Minister Clement Attlee, one of the most powerful political figures in England, in heading a delegation to Soviet Russia and Communist China was a direct slap in the face of the United States, and reflects the unreasoning anti-American feeling which now pervades an influential segment of the British population.

The anti-American London *Mirror,* whose 4,000,-000-reader circulation makes it a power in England, has declared that three out of five Britishers are unfriendly to the United States, or are indifferent.

"We hate being dependent on Uncle Sam," the *Mirror* explained. "We distrust your stability, judgment and experience. We don't like the way you push us around."

This from a country whose safety is being aided day and night by American-manned and-equipped air bases, with 70,000 Americans (including families) swallowing the inhospitality while standing guard.

When we recross the Atlantic and come closer to home we find the same widespread hostility churning up in Latin-American countries.

Although Central and South America have been on the receiving end of American handouts since the establishment of Nelson Rockefeller's Coordinatorship of Inter-American Affairs in 1940, we have not won their fidelity. Latin Americans have taken our money but they have been soured by the knowledge that other countries (notably the ex-enemies, Germany and Japan) were getting much more. They hear no call for gratitude.

This smoldering ill-will flared out at the Inter-American Conference at Caracas when Mexico and Argentina both declined to follow the United States lead and vote for an anti-Communist resolution. It was later reflected in Mexican leadership in the United Nations move against the United States over the Puerto Rican issue. More recently it flared up dangerously in Guatemala, prodded directly by Moscow. It has also made its appearance in Brazil in the overthrow of the late President Vargas.

It is a grim reflection that the United States had given the Latin-American countries, since 1940, $1,270,-000,000 in aid and loans.

In Asia, the snowballing anti-Americanism has already spilled over into action. The Far East nations which we have aided most lavishly are in the forefront of the hostility.

One new Asiatic country which should be bound to

us with hoops of steel is Indonesia. It was the United States, through the Renville Agreement, which literally forced the Netherlands to give Indonesia its independence in 1948, when the Dutch were still on top militarily. In the face of this fact, Indonesia has consistently aligned itself against the United States and with the neutralist bloc in the Southeast Asia power struggle.

After the United States had given Indonesia $207,000,-000 in direct aid and an Import-Export Bank loan of $100,000,000, her press and opinion leaders set up such a shrill outcry—screaming that America was trying to bribe her—that we were forced to withdraw our MSA establishment from the country in 1952.

Now let's look at India.

India has received $278,000,000 in aid from the United States since she won her independence and is due to receive over $100,000,000 more in fiscal 1955. Yet she has constituted herself the spearhead of every Asian anti-American move in the United Nations. In America's fateful struggle with Red China, India has backstopped the Communists at every juncture. She openly displayed her anti-Americanism by welcoming Chou En-lai to India as a conquering hero after he had humiliated the U. S. at Geneva.

What about Japan?

In every discussion of Asia, over-optimistic Americans always bring up Japan as a reassuring hope. Unfortunately, even here we are engaged in specious wishful thinking.

Japan has received $2,439,000,000 in direct aid from

the United States since she surrendered to General Douglas MacArthur in Tokyo Bay; and she has been sheltered from ever-threatening Soviet aggression by the presence of powerful American army, navy and air units, maintained at a cost of further American billions. But millions of her people are astir with anti-American feeling.

Under the deceptive façade of the pro-American Yoshida government, popular anti-Americanism inspired by Communists runs rife in Japan. On May Day, 1954, an estimated 1,600,000 Japanese participated in nationwide anti-U. S. demonstrations. Incendiary banners appeared on the streets, and in the hands of demonstrators before American offices, flaunting: "Yankee, Go Home! Monkey, Go Home!"

Not long ago the moderate Tokyo daily, *Asahi,* conducted an opinion poll on American relations. Almost half of those questioned declared in favor of outright withdrawal of American armed forces from the archipelago. Only 27 per cent favored continued American presence.

And even Canada!

The one country which should be closest to the United States in its world outlook is the Dominion of Canada. We share an unguarded frontier; we are linked to each other by economic and cultural ties which reach intimately into our mutual relationships.

It is a measure of our corroding foreign prestige that even our Canadian relations have shown signs of deterioration. In such international arenas as the United Nations, and in the tense debate over Far East policy,

Canada has been conspicuously drawing away from us in late years. It has been at times an inactive or critical ally in both the Korean and the Indo-China situations. Prime Minister Louis St. Laurent shocked America by a public statement at Manila early in 1954 that Canada must be "realistic" and must recognize the Peiping Communist regime as the government which "the people of China want."

Canadian Foreign Minister Lester B. Pearson voiced the changed Canadian attitude when he declared, in 1951, that "the days of relatively easy and automatic political relations with our neighbor are, I think, over."

This is the dark backdrop of international dislike against which the United States conducts its foreign relations today.

At any time prior to 1914, such American unpopularity abroad might have saddened the American people, but it would not have worried them.

We were a self-sufficient people. Washington's oft-quoted admonition to avoid European entanglements was the watchword of our foreign policy. Our commitments overseas (aside from this hemisphere) were confined to such innocuous international undertakings as the Universal Postal Union. We thought instinctively in terms of national interest, not of international responsibility.

For better or worse, events of the last four decades have detached us from this traditional policy. In the war-time phrase of Churchill our affairs have become "mixed" with those of Europe. America has accepted the role, and the fearful dangers, of world power. She has subordinated her foreign policy to the United Nations. Gradually but surely we have been drawn into an entangling net of foreign commitments and responsibilities which have permanently ended our isolation. As these self-imposed responsibilities have grown, so also has grown our peril.

Because we are no longer self-sufficient, the problem of friendly nations abroad is no longer academic. The goodwill of the Free World is a driving "must" for America. In a world which is sharply divided between Communism and Freedom, the unity of the non-Communist nations is a life-and-death issue. Such unity cannot exist in a poisonous atmosphere in which half the world is singing a song of hate against the United States.

One astute observer of international developments, William Philip Simms, veteran foreign editor of the Scripps-Howard newspapers, has graphically pointed up this problem and has courageously suggested a course of action.

"We have been too lavish with our billions and too sparing of our brains," he wrote recently. "Europeans now accept our aid as nothing more than their due, as they cut down on their own efforts, including military service.

"We should reduce drastically our foreign establishments, bring home all but token forces in uniform, repatriate the swarm of Americans in civvies, drop our give-away programs and use some of the taxpayers' money thus saved to make the United States as impregnable as humanly possible.

"I am not suggesting that we 'abandon' our Allies. I am merely suggesting a better way to serve them and us and the free world. . . . Moreover, in the light of today's facts of

life, how much longer are we going to keep putting the national defense cart before the horse? America's first line of
defense is no longer in Europe. It is in Detroit, Pittsburgh,
Washington, New York, in the air over Canada and the
North Pole. And Europe's first line of defense is in the same
place."

Most Americans perceive the truth about our isolation with more or less clarity, but they fail to relate it
to appropriate action. They depend hopefully upon ill-
conceived crisis-provoking propaganda that, all too often,
actually worsens our present unstable international relations. They turn to the mumbo jumbo of psychology
to resolve their perplexities.

No one seriously disputes the fact that telling the
truth about America and Americans to foreigners has a
place, and an important one, in America's international
activities. But that is not the same thing as saying that
its role is primary. It is only one among several decisive
policies which America must explore if it is to survive.
In reality we have been detouring our national energies
into "gee whiz" activities at a critical time when they
should have been focused on more mature and productive tasks.

It has been the tragedy of America that the promoters of propaganda and "cloak-and-dagger" juvenilities
have been able to call the turns in Washington
throughout the post-war years. They have led us up
costly blind alleys of waste and futility. They have sold
their bill of goods to the Eisenhower Administration,
just as they sold it to Truman and Roosevelt. While they
induce us to piddle with their sterile tasks, time for
America is running out.

Toward the end of 1954, General Mark W. Clark, former Far Eastern commander, declared that a "tough" approach to Communism is the best way to prevent another World War. General Clark, who during World War II commanded our forces in North Africa and in Italy, further warned that the prestige of the United States is getting lower and lower in Europe and Asia and that it is high time this country gave more thought to the material and manpower resources of the Western Hemisphere, because "we may have to stand alone against Communism."

There must be a searching re-appraisal of the whole field of American hand-outs to the world and the information efforts that stimulate these activities if we are to discover some of the reasons why America is both disliked and distrusted.

4

Aid Unlimited

If it were decided to declare a national dividend and to present to every family of three in the United States a bonus of $2,100, the total cost to the Treasury would not equal the amount which this nation has given away to foreign countries since 1940.

Such a mass hand-out would be greeted with horrified protest by most self-respecting Americans, and rightly so. And yet Congress has voted an equivalent amount for foreign give-aways. It is a striking instance of the irresponsible thinking of the elected representatives of the American people during these uncertain years.

The total of our benefactions (they are increasing every twelve months) now stands (1955) at $112 billion.

If we pause to estimate the overdue domestic projects—new schools, health, slum clearance, rural rehabilitation, reclamation, power development, etc.—that these billions or a part of them would have bought if we had kept them at home, the foreign aid undertaking assumes a different and less alluring light. The question of whether we can afford our Lady Bountiful role confronts us challengingly as the hourglass of our economy becomes empty.

The trouble with our Washington rulers is that they are now suffering from a strange new disease known as billionitis.

American legislators feel a curious vertigo when they get up into the rarefied heights of billions. They seem to lose all touch with reality. Men who would argue heatedly over a five-cent raise in a subway or bus fare unhesitatingly vote away billions to foreign peoples without scrutiny or serious argument and without a follow-up audit. The fact that the long-suffering American taxpayer must, in the end, foot the bill is inconsequential to the billion-voting mind. His imagination is intoxicated with Marshall Plans, and Mutual Security and Foreign Operations Administrations, and the underwriting of the American standard of living throughout the globe.

Not long ago, an ambitious "One Worlder," Walter P. Reuther, even climbed up into the trillions. He soberly proposed that the United States, over the next century, should earmark *two trillion dollars* for "Aid" for foreign nations.

How did we get this way?

It has been a slow and erosive process, speeded in recent years by a steady parade of synthetic and government-made "emergencies," each leading to deeper descent into billion-dollar statesmanship. Americans still active in public life can remember the shudder which went over the country when we had our first billion-dollar appropriating Congress. It came in the administration of Woodrow Wilson.

We raised our sights slightly when, under Wilson, we entered World War I. The total American bill for this war and its aftermath which resulted in spectacular victory was $66,592,966,000. Recently we spent more than double this amount in war and rearmament costs as a result of the Korean "police action" which ended up in the most humiliating defeat in American history, with 140,000 American casualties.

The dam went down with a crash under Franklin D. Roosevelt. One of the most portentous of FDR's achievements was that he made us a nation of billion-dollar thinkers. When, in 1934, Roosevelt frightened Congress with his demand for $5 billion for the Hopkins-Ickes relief program, he was actually only softening up the American public for what was to come.

The billion era really picked up speed with the un-corking of Lend-Lease in 1940. Even the title was phony. It was neither lend nor lease. Up to this time, government extravagance, where it had existed, had been restricted to domestic spending. We had kept the money at home. Wilson's World War I loans to the Allies were specifically not gifts; they were loans for which we billed the recipients sternly after Armistice Day, and a large portion of which we collected. When our Allies tried to welch, Calvin Coolidge was to give to history the precious observation: "They hired the money, didn't they?"

The Lend-Lease program set a new precedent. Although it was not spelled out at the time, Lend-Lease was turned over with little or no expectation that any substantial part of it would be returned. We had inaugurated the policy of international give-aways.

Before Lend-Lease had run the course, it had cost us $48,674,000,000. Long before its end it had lost all semblance of a lending operation. It had become a program of outright gifts. Nor was its purpose related exclusively to the financing of the war effort. After the war ended, Lend-Lease spendings continued, with $769,-000,000 going to our Allies after V-J Day.

Lend-Lease was the opening wedge to the admittance to the American mind of the fallacy which has done more to bedevil and pervert our foreign policies since 1945 than any other single delusion.

That fallacy is that we can buy the kind of world that we want by outpourings of American dollars. Since 1945, in our relations with other countries, traditional diplomacy has given place to outright subsidization. Like the Roman Empire in its decadence, we have accepted the dangerous idea that we can keep peace in the world by placing all amenable nations on our payroll.

It didn't work for Rome, and it isn't working for us. The concept, of course, is based upon a cynical view of human nature which disregards the basic wellsprings of human action. The Allies took our money but they were not bought. When we needed them, as in Korea, in Indo-China, and elsewhere, they coldly reserved their individual right of decision. We found that we had subsidized not Allies but neutralists.

As we shall see, much of the smoldering unfriendliness to the United States that exists in Europe and

Asia stems from this mistaken Roosevelt-Truman policy of buying friendship; and to this unsound idea President Eisenhower seems to adhere. Nations proud in the traditions of a long and glorious national history resent the implicit contempt in the American aid attitude. They accept our money, but they don't like the giver.

Once we accepted the subsidization thesis, the giveaway program became a non-stop enterprise. Lend-Lease flickered out in 1946, but it left UNRRA* in its place to continue the spendings. The true UNRRA story has never been told; because UNRRA was an international agency, its records are beyond the subpoena and reach of Congressional investigating committees.

Ostensibly UNRRA was financed jointly by the allied powers. Actually Uncle Sam again picked up the check. Our UNRRA spendings totalled $2,671,000,000. After it was disbanded, we were induced to allocate nearly a third of a billion dollars more to wind up its operations. With a total disregard of our national interests, UNRRA money was unreservedly given to the Communist-ruled nations behind the Iron Curtain. It fed discontented peoples and strengthened the Red grip on their governments. In the Far East, UNRRA money was even allocated to Mao Tse-tung to feed the Communist-occupied regions of China, and to harden Communist rule.

The real successor to Lend-Lease, however, was the Marshall Plan. Initially, this Plan had the objective of strengthening the Free World against Communism. In its first form, American money was to go to Russia and to the Iron-Curtain countries, as well as to the Free Nations. Had the Russians been more farsighted they

* United Nations Relief and Rehabilitation Administration.

would have taken our money, with their fingers crossed, to add to the $11 billion which they had gotten from us through Lend-Lease, using it to strengthen their military potential.

But Russia in 1947 had other irons in the fire, and closed the door to the Marshall Plan for herself and her satellites. The Free Nations eagerly embraced the Plan, and up to December 31, 1951, they had annexed $10,-717,000,000 of American money for "Economic and Technical Assistance," and an additional $2,046,000,000 for "Military Aid."

The Marshall Plan then merged with its successor, Mutual Security Administration. Under MSA, up to January 1, 1954, $16,231,700,000 in additional American money was appropriated exclusively for military aid to the Free Nations, of which $7,700,000,000 represented actual shipments, and the remainder piled up on MSA books as unexpended balance to be spent in the future.

The above totals are exclusive of a long list of other allocations of American money to various foreign aid projects. They do not include the initial Greek-Turkish aid, Chinese stabilization funds, refugee assistance, Philippine rehabilitation, Korean rehabilitation, surplus property grants, Inter-American aid, etc. They do not include the $3,750,000,000 British loan, the $3,266,000,-000 Export-Import Bank Loans, or the $6,252,000,000 item of "Civilian Supplies" outside the UNRRA spendings.

The flow of American money abroad since 1945 has been a reckless and unregulated river. The astronomical sums to which these spendings have mounted stagger the imagination. Uncle Sam has been the great international Easy Touch to whom the whole non-Communist world has come in urgent parade for its share of the pickings.

All this has been done in the name of winning friendship for America. The price has been colossal, but still we have not won the friends. Like the proverbial parvenu we have tried heavy-handedly to buy our way into world leadership. We have not succeeded, but we have piled up a legacy of ill-will throughout the world and a back-breaking debt at home which is now returning to haunt us.

Side by side with these cruder money spendings, some of our Washington wise men have also been endeavoring to apply psychology to the troubled situation. Their well-meant efforts have been just as disastrous to the good name of the United States abroad.

Now let's look at some of the crackpot "win-friends" programs which the United States has sponsored overseas, in the name of psychology.

5

We Go Overboard for Psychological Warfare

Each age has its cherished delusion. Once accepted, the delusion becomes fixed in the social mind—beyond examination and beyond questioning. In our own times the great intellectual booby-trap has become psychological warfare.

The psychology boys are all over the political lot these days. They rule the grand strategy of the political parties in Presidential campaigns. They write and edit the major Presidential speeches. They sit at the elbows of Cabinet officers, of the National Security Council, the Board of Economic Advisers, and Pentagon Brass. Through their minds are winnowed most of the important policy decisions of Washington.

The psychologists got their foothold in Washington under Roosevelt and Truman. But they have really taken over and rule the roost under Eisenhower. Now, as never before, Republican Washington swarms with mysterious figures with strings of degrees behind their names and with the impressive jargon of pseudo-scientific claptrap on their tongues. With their charts and graphs and samplings and social fields and constructs and variables, they mystify the layman and deepen the national confusion. They have made psychological warfare a major Washington industry.

For their ascendancy during the Cold War years there are two outstanding reasons. One is the apparent ability of the psychologists to resolve all the baffling perplexities of the age by one simple, comprehensible answer. The other is the fact that they operate at all times in the realm of the intangible. Their statements and generalizations are not subject to the hard test of the measuring rod and the social caliper. They must be taken on faith. The public has no way of catching up with their boners.

When we are confused and troubled in mind the political quack finds a waiting audience. Today, confusion is endemic and men everywhere are searching frantically for wise men to tell them what it all means. The political psychologist with his glib omniscience has stepped confidently into the prophet role.

And there is just a sufficient tincture of truth in his double talk to make it plausible to the layman.

A hasty run-down of the genealogy of the present Psyk-war (Psychological Warfare) agencies throws a revealing light upon the performance sheets of the psychological warriors in past world political situations.

Paradoxically, the psychological warfare idea, which is now so sternly anti-Communist, sprouted initially in the minds of the "Liberals" of the Thirties and Forties. As they conceived it, psychological warfare was a weapon to be used against Hitler. Few of the pioneers ever contemplated its use against Russia.

The first important forerunner of the present Psykwar establishment was the Institute of Propaganda Analysis of the late Thirties. Its angel was the late Edward A. Filene. The Institute did an elaborate job exposing alleged British propaganda in America and ridiculing the Committee on un-American Activities. But it was less vocal on Russian propaganda, then at its peak in this country. Clyde R. Miller, its executive head and founder, was listed as a sponsor of the Communist-controlled American League for Peace and Democracy.

The Institute faded after Pearl Harbor, but the intellectuals who were specializing in Psykwar found ready berths in the official and semi-official war propaganda agencies. There they spent as much energy in denouncing the so-called Red-baiters who were trying to alert the nation to the after-war Communist peril, as they did in promoting the war effort.

One of the war-time catch-alls for these gentry, Short Wave Research, was forerunner of the present Voice of America. Short Wave Research purported to beam Allied propaganda to the Axis countries. Although under private operation, it tapped the Office of War Information for a subsidy of approximately $500,000. Its secretary, Edward C. Carter, was also Secretary General of the Institute of Pacific Relations during the period when it was slanting its China publications in favor of the Chinese Communists; he was also the President of Russian War Relief and a recipient from Stalin of the Order of the Red Banner of Labor.

Late in the War the whole staff of Short Wave Research was transferred in a body to the OWI.

Another private organization which paved the way for the present Psykwar agencies was the Council for Democracy, later rechristened Citizens for Victory. An interventionist propaganda outfit before Pearl Harbor, and a hunter of alleged pro-Nazis and lukewarm Congressmen thereafter, the Council was heavily supported by important financial contributors. It comes into our story because some of the later Psykwar "experts" cut their eye teeth in Council activities.

Prominent among these was C. D. Jackson,* who was named by President Eisenhower in 1953 as top United States adviser on psychological warfare.

The principal concentration of Psykwar during the war years was in the two government propaganda agencies—the Office of War Information, headed by Elmer Davis, and the Office of Strategic Services, headed by General William J. Donovan. Both agencies, although effective in some phases of the war effort, proved to be disappointing when it came to the all-important job of safeguarding the United States against a hostile postwar Russia.

Although the OWI and OSS heads were selected because of their supposed political acumen, neither Davis nor Donovan appeared to have any inkling of the fierce rivalry which would develop between Soviet Russia and the United States after the war, nor did they take precautions against it. On the contrary, both surrounded themselves with persons who were notoriously soft on the Communist issue, and who went in heavily for eu-

* Succeeded in December 1954 by Nelson A. Rockefeller.

logization of Russia during and after Stalingrad. Their
activities were curtain raisers for Yalta and Potsdam.

The OWI was in continuous hot water throughout
the war because of public distrust of its wide-ranging
efforts.

At one time, the Committee on Un-American Activities staff made an unofficial estimate that between 500
and 600 individuals with un-American connections were
on the OWI rolls. In 1943, Representative Fred E. Bus-
bey of Illinois offered a resolution calling for a Congressional investigation of subversives in the OWI. He
submitted the names and dossiers of 22 alleged
Communists, then on the OWI staff. At one juncture
the House was so fed up with the performance that it
virtually wiped out the OWI appropriation, although
Administration pressure restored it in the Senate.

The unreal atmosphere in which the OWI operated
was shown by its monumental blunders in the Far East
—blunders which we have since paid for in blood and
treasure. With no apparent recognition of the deadly
danger which would confront America if China went
Communist, OWI placed its Far East facilities throughout the war in the hands of men who were on record
for public sympathy with the Chinese Communists.

The OSS, as a hush-hush operation, was better able to
hide its mistakes under the saving shroud of "military secrecy." Some of the facts have leaked out. They reveal a
confused, hastily put together, amateurish organization,
operating largely under its own direction with account-
ancy only to the President, and with an almost unlim-
ited drawing account. Its program was a hodgepodge of
strange odds and ends of psychological warfare coupled
with espionage.

OSS's major mistake was its shortsighted policy of ignoring the after-war role of a victorious Soviet Russia. Its aid was given to Communist activities in the resistance movements of Italy and France. The formidable present French and Italian Communist parties are the tragic consequence of encouragement and support which OSS gave to such Red leaders as Togliatti during the last two years of the war. The incredible Major Holohan case in Italy opened a revealing window on what was happening in both Italy and France in the decisive years of 1943 and 1944.

Many OSS officers operated in a realm of political unreality during the closing war months. Effective work they were doing against the Nazis was cancelled by the amazing blindness with which they served the after-war ends of Stalin.

Meanwhile the Armed Forces themselves were participating directly in psychological warfare work. The line of demarcation between Army and Navy Psykwar on the one hand and the activities of the OWI and the OSS on the other was never clearly drawn; all three groups intermeshed their efforts throughout the war.

In the European Theater, a joint Psychological Warfare Division was set up by the Americans and the British in SHEAF. Operating directly under General Eisenhower, PWD was headed by Brig. General Robert A. McClure. Deputy under McClure was the ubiquitous Jackson who really ran the show. Field units of the PWD accompanied every Allied army; their task was to wage a continuous and imaginative offensive against enemy morale. For their weapons they used the radio, the loud-speaker and the leaflet dropped in huge quantities from planes behind the enemy lines. Unquestionably, the sheer force of this continuous effort during the height of a hot war, directed at enemy soldiers, was effective; it whittled away enemy confidence and will to fight.

General Eisenhower himself, at first dubious over the value of all this activity, paid a warm tribute to Psykwar after V-E Day: "I am convinced that the expenditure of men and money in wielding the spoken and written word was an important contributing factor in undermining the enemy's will to resist and supporting the fighting morale of our potential allies in the occupied countries."

In the Pacific Theater, where the Japanese were scoring successes with their persuasive Greater East Asia Co-Prosperity propaganda, effective counter work was set up. Here the most notable name was that of Admiral Ellis M. Zacharias whose broadcasts across the Japanese lines were an amazing tour de force.

The end of the war found a whole new profession of psychological warfare experts—trained in the OSS, the OWI and the Army and Navy Psykwar units—with no place to go. They became vociferous clamorers for a continuance of a large-scale foreign propaganda program in peace time. Recognizing that Congress was in no mood to make appropriations for their autonomous continuance, they accepted the second best, a transfer to the State Department. On August 31, 1945, President Truman issued an Executive Order shifting the overseas functions of the OWI and the OIAA (which served Latin America) to the International Information Service of the State Department. At the same time, the OSS was dissolved and 1,000 of its personnel were moved into the new Intelligence Section of the Department. Directing this new State Department agency was William Benton, Assistant Secretary of State for Public Affairs; under Benton, William T. Stone was appointed head of the International Information Service.

In view of their background, it would be difficult to find two more unfortunate choices for peace-time Psykwar activities. Benton, after a successful career in the advertising business, had fallen under the influence of the "One World" ideas of Chancellor Robert M. Hutchins at the University of Chicago. With his former partner, Chester Bowles, Benton had aligned himself with the radical left wing of the Democratic Party.

William T. Stone, before joining the government, had been one of the members of the editorial board of the discredited magazine *Amerasia* from 1937 through 1941, including the whole period of the Hitler-Stalin Pact of 1939-41. After Stone's record was examined, the State Department Security Office recommended on March 22, 1946, that his resignation from the Department be arranged. Benton kept Stone on the job, and Stone was later promoted to the post of special assistant to Edward W. Barrett, one of Benton's successors; he was not eased out of the Department until 1952, after an investigating Senate Committee had given him adverse publicity.

Under such top direction, it was inevitable that the International Information Service should develop an indulgent soft-headedness toward our relations with the Soviet. The OWI and OSS leftovers from the war period, heavy with infiltrators who believed Stalin would be our post-war partner in the world peace, were trans-

ferred *in toto* to the State Department payroll in 1946.
Most of the 284 security risks which were reported to
Secretary Byrnes by the Security officers in 1946, and
which Byrnes noted in his oft-quoted letter to Congressman Adolph J. Sabath, were OWI and OSS transferees.
Most of them were still on the rolls in 1948 when a
House Appropriations subcommittee made a searching
investigation of subversives in the State Department. A
surprisingly large number were still drawing pay as late
as 1950 when the subject again was sensationally aired.

Not until the Cold War had been clarified in the
public mind by exhaustive public discussion, did the
USIS*, the Voice of America, and the other information
agencies under Benton and his successors grasp the fact
that the world Communist conspiracy was the enemy.
The Psykwar agencies throughout 1946, 1947 and even
as late as 1948 executed a masterful straddle of the actual issues which were facing America in its increasing
rupture with the Kremlin. Their offices throughout the
world were manned by amiable misfits who avoided con-
troversy and endeavored to scatter sweetness and light.
Their interpretations of American public opinion were
tailored to the partisan twists and turns of the Administration's hand-washing in the face of Communist aggression. The millions which they squandered were sheer
waste, in terms of any actual betterment of the American picture abroad.

Psychological warfare had won acceptance as a permanent peace-time function of the nation, but its voice had
proved to be feeble and ineffectual.

* United States Information Service.

6

To Mold Men's Minds?

For the first time in history, American propagandists and cultural promoters abroad have become almost as numerous as our accredited diplomatic representatives and their staffs. Today our psychological warriors occupy almost as much office space and housing facilities as do our diplomats. Often these USIA* press agents, whose aim it is to "mold men's minds," impede and disrupt important moves to carry out established diplomatic procedures.

Since the end of the shooting phase of World War II, our Government's overseas establishment and payroll have grown beyond reason and usefulness. Visualize, if you can, the entire population of Columbus, Ohio; or Newark, New Jersey; or Memphis, Tennessee, or Oakland, California, and you will have a rough idea of the

* United States Information Agency.

number of civilians employed by the U. S. Government
throughout the world.

Have you ever seen a crowd of half a million people
in one place and at one time? Our overseas payroll army
is bigger than that.

Foreigners generally are amazed at the lavish expenditures of the FOA, the USIA, and other grossly overstaffed United States agencies abroad. They cannot understand how the American people, who pay the bills,
can continue to tolerate these ostentatious spendings—
a performance in plain view of the tens of thousands of
American tourists who annually travel in Europe.

Paris is a striking case in point. The U. S. Government is the sole occupant of a dozen impressive buildings in the heart of Paris. This glamorous city of love,
laughter and light has become the American Capital
of Europe—the Europe that Uncle Sam still has a multi-
billion-dollar urge to preserve.

In all the world no headquarters for press agents enjoys more regal surroundings than those occupied by
the USIA in the block-long Paris chateau that once
belonged to Baron Rothschild. The historic building,
with its formal gardens and an entrance on the re-
nowned Rue du Faubourg St. Honoré, adjoins the
British Embassy. Moreover, it is as large as the entire
Diplomatic headquarters of Her Britannic Majesty's
Government in France.

But our elaborate French chateau for press agents is
only one of three big buildings devoted exclusively to
Uncle Sam's "cultural bombardment" in Paris. Across
the street from the main American Embassy building
in the famed Place de la Concorde is the once re-

nowned Café des Ambassadeurs restaurant and night club building, a long two-story structure facing the gardens of the lower Avenue Champs Élysées. This great building, like the Chateau Rothschild, is tenanted entirely by USIA payrollers. A third building, the Hotel Astoria, once one of the ultra-de luxe hotels of Europe and situated at the top of the Avenue Champs Élysées in the exclusive Étoile district, is the headquarters of the USIA library.

Our propagandists, and those who sponsor their activities, take special pride in boasting about the "cultural relations" maintained through the U. S. Information Agency's overseas libraries. In Paris, for example, we maintain a large government-operated library. In addition to this main library, the USIA maintains half a dozen branch libraries in that many French cities.

The one thing which we definitely don't need in France is any more libraries. For the USIA found a superb American library system in full operation in France when it came upon the scene. In 1920, the American Library of Paris became the largest single United States cultural enterprise ever operated overseas, on the basis of strictly private support. This worthy enterprise, supported by American Friends of France, maintains branches in six other French cities. French men and women borrow from it more than 400,000 books per year. This free-enterprise program to promote culture in France accomplishes more in cementing and furthering Franco-American relations than all of our costly propaganda efforts. Moreover, it offers ample proof that the U. S. Information Agency's library setup is sheer duplication, as well as a poor imitation, of an honest and unselfish effort conceived and maintained by American citizens for more than thirty-three years, and without political fanfare, waste and corruption.

In Paris, too, many Frenchmen complain bitterly of brand new American housing projects along both sides of the Seine. A $5,000,000 housing development, with hundreds of completely furnished apartments, has been erected with American taxpayers' money for the sole occupancy of our government's payrollers (residents) in the French capital. These are dubbed by the French, "Ike's eyesores." The housing development has in one area reduced the values of adjoining property, a circumstance that hardly makes for the betterment of Franco-American relations! Furthermore, the French quite properly feel that the décor is more in keeping with that of Las Vegas than of Paris, which they want to preserve as the most beautiful city in the world.

If the United States were benefiting in goodwill from this ostentation and spending, we might overlook the lapses in good taste and tact. Unfortunately, the reverse is the case. As the information outlays have burgeoned, the curve of American popularity has gone steadily downward in both France and Italy (which is another scene of opulent American spending). We are like a man on a revolving wheel: the more money we spend, the faster the wheel propels us backwards.

The real humiliation of the situation is that while we pour out billions, and become more disliked, Soviet Russia spends comparatively little, directly, in both France and Italy, and yet its influence proliferates. The explanation of course is that Russia does not send armies of conspicuous Russian propagandists to these countries; her propaganda is conducted for her by native French and Italian Communists. Russia has no need to maintain princely edifices for its propagandists, like the Chateau Rothschild, because she has highly trained native Reds, in her Communist parties, who skilfully plead Russia's case as Frenchmen and Italians—and not as outsiders.

Undoubtedly the Ducloses and the Togliattis receive some form of subsidy from Moscow. But, ironically, the major part of the money which is used in those countries to blast the United States is contributed by native French and Italians in the form of dues and contributions. The Communist propaganda apparatus, in the free world countries, instead of being a drain upon Russia is actually a source of revenue.

These native Communists are particularly effective because they have developed the art of playing domestic demagogic politics to a fine point.

French and Italian Red leaders don't waste time talking about ideology, outside the leadership circles. When they appeal to the common people they talk the bread and butter language of day-to-day demands. Like a Tammany or Pendergast club house a Communist headquarters is a place to which the little people can come and get friendly advice and aid in their personal problems.

Communist leaders make themselves close to the common people in their mode of life and their every appeal. In contrast to this intimate human touch, America's FOA and USIA, with their exalted, intellectualized talk and action, seem far away and remote from the people. The fact that the ruthless, bloody-

handed Kremlin is behind Communist welfarism is neither apparent nor consequential to the average low-income Frenchman or Italian.

As the late Alcide de Gasperi told Mr. Gabriel
Vogliotti, a correspondent of *Collier's:*

"They [the Communists] have made themselves look and
sound reasonable. The Communists have stolen the copy-
right on reforms; they have convinced millions that they
have the only real concern for the poor; they have dropped
their wild-eyed, bomb-throwing revolutionary tactics. They
preach moderation. They urge 'sensible' tax laws and no
longer rave about the rich. Their deputies make speeches
on land reform that sound like kindly advice from wise
uncles. When a government agency grants a wage increase
the Communists claim the credit for getting it. They pose
as the only party fighting for popular education, redistribu-
tion of land, new housing and labor reforms."

The American propaganda set-up in Italy is almost
as fantastic as in France. In Italy we can gasp in disbelief
at the exhibition of United States outlays, both in personnel and buildings in historic Rome. On the fashionable Via Vittoria Veneto looms a block-long seven-story
edifice. This building, once a great luxury hotel, now
houses the activities of America's FOA and USIA.

Adjacent to the former hotel, and on the same broad
avenue, is a second USIA building—the library. Almost
directly across the street is the former U. S. Embassy,
now merely a place to have documents authenticated
—a U. S. Consul's office. Separated from the larger
former Embassy building by a formal royal garden,
complete with marble steps and priceless Italian statu-

ary, is our present United States Embassy. This was once the home of the Queen Mother of Italy.

No other nation in the world occupies for its Embassy an edifice of such magnificence: in appearance and size it resembles London's Buckingham Palace. To the left of this colossal building is a block-long private parking lot that was once a royal garden. At one end of this enclosure is a fifty-car garage, complete with a corps of Italian chauffeurs in constant attendance to serve VIP residents and visitors, and directly across from the garage is still another building, as large as our original Embassy in Rome. It is tenanted entirely by high officials of the United States Information Agency!

To the uninitiated it would appear that this ostentatious grandeur must be the setting for extremely effective American operations, justifying such lavish expense. Unfortunately, almost the reverse is true. We are tragically losing ground in Italy. Despite American giveaways in the billions, and propaganda in the millions, the Communist Party in Italy gained nearly a quarter of a million new members in 1953.

The hard-pressed American taxpayer continues, year after year and under the administration of both political parties, to accept the staggering costs of the FOA and its junior companion, the USIA, on the earnest assurance of the top brass in Washington and their understudies overseas that they are doing far-reaching things to halt the advance of Communism on the economic, psychological and informational fronts. If Italy is an example, then the record is indeed a shameful one.

In Italy, from 1948 to 1953, USIA and its predecessor

organization, USIS, were continually operative with a program practically identical with its present one and masterminded by the same Regional Director and personnel! But, far from checking Communist growth in Italy, the joint Communist-Red Socialist parliamentary strength in Italy increased during this five-year period from 31 per cent to 35 per cent. And still worse, discerning observers generally agree today (early in 1955) that the Communist-Red Socialist coalition is now so near to power that there is an acute danger that the Italian people will vote themselves into Communism at a parliamentary election in the not distant future.

From the American point of view, the rightward swing of another large bloc of Italian voters in the 1953 parliamentary elections offered equally sobering reflection upon the efficacy of American propaganda in Italy. While the democratic Center parties, which we favor and help to promote, were losing 1,171,000 to the Communist-Red Socialists, they were simultaneously losing 2,142,000 votes to the anti-American right wing parties which were once Monarchist or Fascist. Such a defection was a staggering verdict upon the results of American give-aways and their propaganda support in Italy—even though backed by $3,500,000,000 of American Marshall Plan and MSA aid.

This is not the full story.

The maladministration and waste of both personnel and money in our Government's huge and far-flung propaganda activities are not confined to France and Italy; they are duplicated throughout Europe, the Near East, South America and parts of the Orient still free from Red China. Too few Americans realize that the USIA is today spending millions and its chief spokesmen are still seeking to obtain more millions to waste in countries where we should not be spending one dollar for propaganda—countries like Turkey, Greece, Belgium, the Netherlands, the Scandinavian countries, Great Britain and Spain, where the Communist menace is so remote that it simply does not justify our attempts to "mold men's minds." The majority of the peoples of these countries understand the menace of Communism and want no part of it.

In this connection, it may be revealing to Americans unfamiliar with our Government's spending for propaganda in parts of the world where it is neither needed nor wanted, to review the testimony and questioning of the head propaganda director on the occasion of his appearance before a House Appropriations subcommittee in 1954. Let's begin with a question concerning Spain, asked by Congressman Cliff Clevenger (Rep., Ohio), Chairman of the subcommittee.

MR. CLEVENGER: As to Spain, where we have no present Communist problem, I hope it will be happier than it is in Italy and France where we have not only spent a large amount of money but put forth other efforts. Have you been in this long enough to have an answer for me on this: If you sent a comparable mission to the one which went to Latin America, is there any section of the world where you believe they would report we were not spread too thin? I have been sitting here ever since this agency was created and I have seen it reorganized 5 or 6 times. I have yet to have presented to us any concrete agreement of the information agencies.

MR. STREIBERT: What you want is where we think we may

be over-staffed and over-programmed. There are such areas, yes.

MR. CLEVENGER: I want to know whether I, as an American, in a country in the financial situation we are in now, and where it is so desperately necessary to balance our budget, whether I can further justify the spending of the vast sums of money asked for. Your request is as big as that of the State Department. At one time they asked for nearly a quarter of a billion dollars for 1 year's operation. Did you know that?

MR. STREIBERT: No.

MR. CLEVENGER: The budget Bureau gave them $170 million, which we succeeded in cutting back to some $87 million. I have been on this thing ever since the Bureau was organized. Is there any concrete performance you can put your finger on and say "They did this for the United States Government."

MR. STREIBERT: May I go off the record for a moment?

MR. CLEVENGER: Yes.

(Discussion held off the record.)

MR. COUDERT (Rep., N. Y.): The Director, Mr. Chairman, has referred to Spain. For the first time we have an arrangement whereby we are going to spend perhaps $1 billion in the near future in Spain for the acquisition of bases and construction of military installations. We are going to evidently maintain substantial military forces in Spain. Spain is clearly not in danger of being overrun by internal Communists. Yet in your budget request you increase your request for funds to be used for propaganda in Spain by almost a third, $198,000. I would be interested in some more precise justification as to why we have to explain to the Spanish at our own expense why we are there. Obviously we are there with the consent of their Government. We are building bases there. I am sure questions will be asked as to why we have to go to even additional cost, however modest, relatively speaking, to explain to them why we are doing it.

MR. STREIBERT: Well, in places where we have bases and troops we always have a basic problem of getting support from the populace of the area so as not to have agitation about getting United States troops out of a friendly country and bases discontinued. We always have that opposition.

MR. COUDERT: Why isn't that the responsibility of the local government through whose consent troops are invited in and allowed to remain?

MR. STREIBERT: Well, if we left it to them and we lose out it would be too bad for us. We cannot afford to do that. We cannot afford to let any of these local governments in these places completely alone without any reference on our part to its being understood.

MR. COUDERT: Well, that is an interesting point of view. I take it your reasoning also applies, then, to communities such as Great Britain, for which you are budgeting a substantial sum, $832,000. Great Britain is one of our Air Force bases, an integral part of NATO, and yet apparently the Information Service, with the support of the State Department, deems it necessary to spend very large sums of money every year for propaganda in Great Britain. That is to explain why we are there, to explain to the British people apparently what their own government policy is. It seems to me that is a situation which requires a certain amount of justification.

MR. STREIBERT: We are not trying to reach all British people. We are trying to reach the leaders and the influential groups, and the labor union leaders. We want them to support the same policies of Great Britain that are in harmony with ours. We want active support of NATO, for example.

MR. COUDERT: You are undertaking to do the propaganda

job for the British Government? Is that what it amounts to in substance?

MR. STREIBERT: All we hope to do is to identify ourselves with their goals and aspirations, which is, after all, the only thing that ties them to us.

MR. COUDERT: Doesn't the British Government do that themselves?

MR. STREIBERT: Yes.

MR. COUDERT: Does not Churchill make speeches from time to time and very often and very effectively about the importance of maintaining American relations?

MR. STREIBERT: Yes.

MR. COUDERT: Wasn't the Labor Government in power at the time NATO first was conceived?

MR. STREIBERT: Yes.

MR. COUDERT: That is why I think it would be interesting to members of this committee to know what the Information Service does with this money in Great Britain for the purpose of influencing opinion in Great Britain.

MR. STREIBERT: That I will not put on the record.

MR. COUDERT: That is your privilege.

MR. STREIBERT: May I answer it off the record? I have a very complete response to it.

MR. CLEVENGER: I don't like to see discussions off the record on this.

MR. COUDERT: These points I think, Mr. Chairman and Mr. Director, would be interesting to people who read this record. I note that in your various areas you are planning to spend $133,000 in Australia. Australia is part of the British Commonwealth. Australia is an essential element in NATO presumably. Australia is also, I think, a party to our Pacific Defense Treaty. Yet you plan to spend substantial sums of money, $133,000 for the purpose of influencing opinion in Australia. I think that could stand a little more explanation.

In Belgium, also a NATO country, you are planning to spend $319,000. In Denmark, the smallest of the European countries in NATO, you are planning to spend $307,000. Incidentally, all of these items are greater than the sums actually spent in 1954.

In France, where we maintain very substantial military forces, and have constructed military establishments, where tourists by the hundreds of thousands go every summer, where we have the closest relations, cultural, economic, and of every other kind, you are planning to spend $4 million which is an increase of $750,000 over the previous year.

In the Netherlands you are planning to spend a half million dollars.

In New Zealand, you are planning to spend the small sum of $46,000.

We have already referred to Spain, $700,000 to be spent, an increase of nearly $200,000.

Sweden is in for $191,000, an increase of $22,000.

Even in little Switzerland, which certainly I would not suppose needed any explanation of the American position, we are planning to spend $58,000, a substantial increase over the preceding year.

In the Union of South Africa, one of the members of the British Commonwealth, we are planning to spend $115,000, which is a substantial increase.

Mr. Streibert, that runs all through this budget request, as it did the year before. I was very much interested in it then.

MR. STREIBERT: Yes, sir.

MR. COUDERT: What is the population of Hong Kong?

MR. STREIBERT: About 2 million.

MR. COUDERT: You are planning to spend $751,000 in Hong Kong, an increase of nearly $200,000 over the previous year.

In Indo-China, in addition to the enormous sums that we are spending to support the French military effort, you are planning to spend $2 million for explanation of why we are there, an increase of nearly $1 million.

In Indonesia you are planning to spend $864,000, an increase of nearly $250,000.

In South Korea, where hundreds of thousands of American troops have fought and where we have suffered heavy casualties, and where enormous sums of American dollars and resources and manpower have been used for reconstruction, you think it necessary to spend $1,600,000 in round figures, an increase of nearly $460,000 "in order," to use the well-chosen words of my good friend Mr. Coon from Oregon last year, "to tell them why we are there."

In Malaya, a British Crown Colony, you are planning to spend $772,000, an increase of $269,000.

This goes right down through the various areas of the world.

When you come to the Near East—

MR. BOW (Rep., O.): Will you yield?

MR. COUDERT: Yes.

MR. BOW: In Thailand I think we found some of the most friendly people to the United States.

MR. COUDERT: I overlooked that at the bottom of the list. In Thailand you are planning to spend nearly $2 million, which is an increase of $1 million over the current fiscal year, which in the light of my friend Mr. Bow's observation I think is interesting.

Then you come to the Near East, and the first figure that stands out is that for Greece. We have spent enormous sums since the original Turkey-Greece program was initiated in 1949, of every character. Yet you still think it necessary to spend nearly $1 million for explanation to the Greeks why we did it.

India we have already referred to. We have there an increase of nearly $1 million and we plan to spend $3 million. There are several other countries in those areas where it is a little difficult to understand exactly why it should be necessary to spend such substantial sums of moneys to explain the American position.

Later, at the same Congressional hearings, Mr. Streibert made this statement regarding Indo-China:

"You have gone from those countries through many critical areas, areas positively at war. I can testify from personal knowledge of why the increase in Indo-China. We want to win the war there. I think it is important. We are engaged in psychological warfare, in effect, in our informational activities there. Our purposes there are to promote the support of the Vietnamese army by the Vietnamese people. *We assist in promoting recruiting for the army*. We get out an immense amount of effective posters and literature, and we are trying to get the war won there.

"You may well say that is the responsibility of the French and the Vietnamese.

"On the other hand, the Vietnamese are very anxious to have us teach them how to carry on these psychological warfare methods.

"They are unfamiliar with them."

Unfortunately, the last five words of testimony proved, in the course of tragic events, to be absolutely true.

Throughout the world we witness the sad spectacle of overstaffed and ineffective propaganda offices; of unrestrained outpouring of American taxpayers' money on callow, unproductive and all too often harmful in-

formation projects, and of steadily dwindling goodwill
for the United States in the countries where the dollars
are being spent.

We shall have few digressions into statistics in this
book, but there are some situations whose dimensions
can only be pointed up by cold figures.

We can comprehend the size of the information bear
which we have by the tail when we note that in fiscal
1954 a total of 10,171 persons were on the USIA payroll
in Washington, D. C., and in its 77 overseas missions.
The average annual salary which they drew, according
to the 1954 budget report, aggregated $5,735.

A comparison of USIA's ten thousand payrollers with
the streamlined personnel of an efficient private news-
gathering organization of comparable scope will show
how ridiculously overstaffed USIA is.

Consider the New York *Times*. It publishes a huge
daily edition, and a Sunday edition which, with its supplements, runs to several hundred pages per copy. Its
news facilities reach into every part of the world.

And yet this immense publishing enterprise gets out
its issues with a total editorial and news staff of approximately 325 persons.

The Chicago *Tribune,* boasting the largest circulation of any standard-size daily newspaper published in
the United States, employs a staff of about 282 people
for its local, neighborhood, domestic and foreign coverage of the news.

Twenty-five leading American newspapers in all sections of the United States have a *combined* total of
only 5,000 employees in their editorial and news de-

partments. The Associated Press, with correspondents throughout the world to serve its member newspapers in the United States and its clients abroad, maintains its very extensive day and night wire services with a total of 3,000 employees.

USIA's heavy payrolls unquestionably indicate an extremely unhealthy administrative situation.

What *do* the 10,171 in our government's super-press agency really do?

One highly exploited USIA effort is its international press service. In the 1954 budget, $4,220,288 was allotted to this purpose. USIA prepares in Washington, D. C., and sends out a 6,000-word daily wireless bulletin which goes to all United States missions abroad for release to the foreign press.

What actually happens to most of this rush rush news? All too often it ends up only as a poster on the walls or a give-away on reception room tables of high-rent USIA headquarters and other U. S. Government offices overseas. Unfortunately, the number of native people who read and believe this "made in the U. S. Information Agency" news barrage is pitifully small. Has it perhaps occurred to the Agency's Washington managers that air mail would be speedy enough for these 6,000-word-long, five-day-a-week propaganda bulletins?

Moreover, by any commercial press association yardstick, the USIA output, with its background supplements by unknown news commentators, appears dull and amateurish. It duplicates inefficiently what such organizations as the Associated Press, the United Press and the International News Service do with practical

professional skill in serving the newspapers of the
United States and the world. The USIA bulletins perform no visible important function that is not expertly
performed by existing non-government agencies.

When the USIA propaganda director and his large
staff of assistant directors and other officials appear before the appropriations committees of the Congress in
their annual appeals for increased funds, they argue that,
without the facilities of the USIA, our country would be
completely isolated insofar as telling the world about
America is concerned. The USIA managers would have
us believe that our great Nation is informationally
blacked out and that they provide the only "open window to the world" for the dissemination of our ideas,
ideals and objectives. In saying this they ignore the immense contribution to overseas understanding of America which is made by private publishing organizations
operating without government subsidy.

For instance, superbly written statements of the
American point of view are printed and distributed
throughout the world by our own *Reader's Digest,* but
with this generally unknown and important difference
—the *Reader's Digest* international editions are published abroad in twelve languages, in thirty different
editions; and the monthly circulation of this fine foreign
promotion *for* Americans totals 7,165,000 copies that
are distributed in 58 countries to reach a monthly
readership of thirty million people!

And the *Reader's Digest* overseas circulation—tremendous as it is—is only a part of the English and foreign language American publications which regularly
enjoy large foreign readership. These include:

Life, foreign and South American editions	550,000 semi-monthly
Saturday Evening Post	425,000 weekly
Time, newsmagazine	375,000 weekly
Newsweek, newsmagazine (American edition)	60,000 weekly
U. S. News and World Report (American edition)	25,000 weekly
Collier's	225,000 semi-monthly
Look Magazine	181,000 semi-monthly

The New York *Times* issues a special overseas air-mail edition. Its daily circulation is 18,000 copies. The weekend New York *Times* overseas edition has a circulation of 31,000 copies. This American newspaper, together with the Paris edition of the New York *Herald Tribune,* published six days a week in the French capital and with a circulation of 52,000 daily, is read by most editors, bankers, industrialists and government officials throughout Europe, the Near East, and South America. Additionally, the London *Times* and *Daily Mail,* together with other leading newspapers published in Great Britain, are distributed throughout Europe and reach tens of thousands of their foreign readers on the continent and elsewhere within hours after publication.

With such powerful private vehicles bringing the American and British points of view to all political leaders and opinion makers throughout the world, it seems singularly needless for the Government of the United States to enter the publication field in rivalry. And yet Uncle Sam shelled out over $4 million in 1954 to maintain the USIA's amateurish press adjunct.

This money was wasted; all American publications,

weekly, semi-monthly and monthly magazines and daily and Sunday newspapers, plus the newspapers from Great Britain, are obtainable at hotel news counters, at railroad stations, in office building news stores and at thousands of news kiosks in all of the principal cities of the world.

A fair question is—what about the publications of Soviet Russia? The answer is "zero" because the "affluent" citizens of the Kremlin are not allowed the freedom of foreign travel and, more important, no Russian is spoken or read outside of the Soviet Union and the countries it has made prisoner.

Always in self-defense, the spokesmen for the U. S. Information Agency like to refer to the large sums which they claim the Soviets spend annually for world propaganda and to compare this with our own (1955) USIA appropriation of $77,000,000 for foreign propaganda. The comparison often seems startling, but it is not the whole story. Our propagandists always neglect to mention that a full comparison would have to include all the private press, magazine, radio and television expenditures made each year throughout the United States; these would exceed the Soviet totals by many billions of dollars.

Another false argument and one frequently made by the USIA pleaders is that England, France, Italy and other European countries spend nearly as much for overseas propaganda as we do. This argument is totally fallacious. The principal European countries, taken together, spend approximately $40 million annually to attract the more than 400,000 Americans who travel abroad each year. This is self-liquidating promotion aimed solely at the generous spending of hundreds of thousands of American vacationists, who form the world's largest and most profitable travel group.

Two other major activities of the USIA which are discussed in detail in the following chapters are the Motion Picture Service and the Voice of America. The Motion Picture Service accounted, in 1954, for $4,065,-251 of the total USIA budget. Voice of America accounted for $17,791,836.

The prize exhibit of the USIA overseas mission is the library which is maintained in most of the important cities. In principal European capitals and in the Near East the USIA libraries and cultural centers are mostly located in fashionable sections where wage earners and poorly clad readers are not welcomed. In such important cities as Paris, Rome and Cairo the libraries are out of bounds for the masses. In Cairo, for example, the library is located behind a high iron fence in the section where the ultra-swank Embassy and skyscraper apartments are. Egyptian soldiers guard the entrance by day and by night. Poorly clad Arab natives do not venture into this part of the Moslem city. Hours are arranged for the convenience of the Americans, not of the native population; libraries are closed evenings when the poorer readers might consult them, and on Saturdays and all holidays. Some libraries are open only three or four hours in the middle of the day.

As a consequence of these ill-considered policies, our overseas libraries with their elaborate main and special reading rooms are notorious as hangouts for the reading and writing convenience of American tourists, rather than for the natives. Thus, through poor administration and wrong location, the primary propaganda purpose of this costly program, which is not duplicated by any other nation, is being frustrated. The libraries cost Uncle Sam more than $4 million annually.

It is important to recall that in 1948 we spent $21 million for foreign propaganda. Today we are spending 5 times that sum and we have fewer foreign friends and supporters than we had then. Today we are still trying to accomplish through torrents of ill-conceived and badly timed propaganda what our nation's leaders and chief spokesmen have failed to accomplish for us through diplomatic efforts.

Chairman Cliff Clevenger (Rep., Ohio), of the House Appropriations subcommittee, while considering the USIA appropriation in the 83rd Congress, voiced the general Congressional skepticism of the Agency, its claims and its operations, when he said: "Attention is called here to the results which have been obtained in proportion to the amount of money we have spent. Where you have spent the most money, there is also the most lamentable condition up until this time, and if someone can explain that away, I would be interested in hearing that."

And the late Senator Pat McCarran (Dem., Nev.) said:

"I have been on this committee for twenty years and I have not seen any results from the money we have expended. I should like to see it now."

"So would I," replied Director Streibert, "it would be very good to have a total measure of results. We just don't have it. We will never get it."

Our government's chief propagandist, perhaps accidentally, gave the correct answer!

A definitive observation on our whole psychological warfare endeavor has been made by one of America's most highly respected opinion leaders.

Mr. Walter Lippmann, the eminent columnist and political commentator, writing from Paris, said in the New York *Herald Tribune* of November 2, 1954:

"What Europeans would like is our firm support of the Atlantic Alliance, and less direct intervention in their internal affairs. They would like us to make the maintenance of the Alliance the great object of our policy, and leave it more to them to determine how to do propaganda and psychological warfare with their own Communists.

"When things take shape after the election we shall have to consider the necessity of removing the irritation caused by our overzealous meddling in the internal affairs of Western Europe. For what we call psychological warfare is, I am persuaded, doing more harm to the United States than it is to the Soviet Union. In the near future we shall have to give it an agonizing reappraisal."

7

Is the Voice <u>for</u> Americans?

The story of the Voice of America is the story of a great enthusiasm and a disappointing fulfillment. It had its beginnings in the exalted "One World" mood which swept over America at the close of World War II.

Everyone realized, in the delirious days of 1945, that in its new role of world leadership, America would desperately need dependable foreign friends. How to win and hold them was the question.

Now there has never been anything occult about the art of gaining foreign friends. Nations make friends through diplomacy. In the traditional procedure, foreign offices get together to create situations of mutuality which will lead to good international relations. It is an exercise in shrewd give and take. It is conducted throughout at the top governmental level.

But full reliance upon such proven procedure was unacceptable in the heightened mentality of V-J Day.

The old diplomacy is obsolete, insisted the "One World-ers." There must be a new diplomacy—the diplomacy of high voltage propaganda. The recognized diplomatic channels must be by-passed. The plea for foreign good-will must be made over the heads of the governments—it must be pointed like a pistol at the people of the entire world! The people, in each country, must be reached by the new wonder-drug techniques of the Voice of America and the USIS.

We are only now awakening to the full absurdity of this 1945 decision. Meanwhile, as America has tink-ered with its ineffective and all too often harmful prop-aganda gadgets, our opportunity to create a world in which Americans can live safely may perhaps have slipped away from us.

For this new gadget approach we started out with a war-time Voice of America, inherited from the OWI. Reluctant to dismantle the Voice, President Truman transferred it to the Department of State. There it sur-vived on a skeleton scale while Congress pondered its future.

What vitality the Voice possessed in the immediate post-war years it owed to the insistence of William Ben-ton, then Assistant Secretary of State. Benton extracted $19 million from Congress for the first after-war year to finance the Voice and all other State Department in-formational programs, under the name International Education Division. In the second year, the appropria-tion was sliced to $13 million. No attempt was made to beam Voice programs to Soviet Russia. The Ameri-can people were still in the war-time trance of faith in Stalin's good intentions, and the necessity of propaganda to sell Americanism to the Soviet was not encouraged.

The Cold War jolted the nation into a different mood. The Truman Doctrine of 1946 and the Soviet rejection of the Marshall Plan in 1947 were eye-opening experiences for Americans. It began to be realized that the peace was an illusion.

Exploiting this new national spirit, Benton went before Congress, with Truman and Marshall backing, and won the enactment of a law giving permanent status to the information program, including the Voice. With the passage of this law, the Smith-Mundt Act, Congress upped the information budget to $30 million. To show that it was in a spending frame of mind, it appropriated an additional $11,320,000 to build overseas booster stations to increase the Voice range. The United States discontinued its attempt to publish and circulate an English language slick magazine, *Amerika,* in Russia, and turned to a new effort to reach the Russian masses, over Stalin's head, by radio.

But the Voice reached its real heyday with the advent of the Korean war. With World War III a nightmarish possibility, Congress was urged to go all out for propaganda. The air was filled with extravagant talk of the possibilities of radio broadcasting. The magazine *Fortune* published an article proposing the jaw-breaking sum of $500,000,000 be appropriated solely for information. Paul G. Hoffman, then director of ECA*, was slightly more conservative; he proposed an annual kitty of a mere $300,000,000! Hoffman recommended that the trifling sum of $45,000,000 of the taxpayers' money be given to the State Department "on a *confidential* ba-

* Economic Cooperation Administration.

sis, free from the need of public disclosure and usable at the *discretion* of the administrator."

Congress, although in a gay handout mood, was not quite so willing. It voted $120,000,000 for the first year following the outbreak of the war in Korea. Voice facilities and personnel zoomed overnight.

The VOA was now rich and all dressed up but it quickly found it had no place to go. It became painfully obvious that the directors of the Voice, once they had their unwarranted and excessive appropriation, had only the haziest notion of what they wanted to do with all of their new found wealth.

Edward W. Barrett, who was now in Benton's old job in the State Department, put on an exciting show of plans and proposed projects, but the follow-through was a painful letdown. Borrowing an idea from semantics, Barrett re-packaged the program, not as "propaganda," but as the "Campaign of Truth." He announced that the United States was going to win the "mind of the world." The reach was magnificent, but the grasp was meager—it flittered into the wild blue yonder, and, to our sorrow, we have been losing instead of winning foreign minds ever since!

One truth which soon became plain was that argumentation proves hollow if it is not backed up by firm and undeviating government action to command and hold the respect of the world. In Secretary Acheson's State Department policies between 1949 and 1953, Mr. Barrett soon learned that he was trying to market an extremely unsalable brand of merchandise. The Asiatic mind was not easily impressed by the VOA assertions when it remembered the questionable role which the United States had played in China in 1948 and 1949.

After the Korean war started, it was hard to sell American war policies to the world when they wobbled from day to day in response to the pressures and the interdicts of the British Labor Party government. When President Truman, yielding to British insistence, fired General Douglas MacArthur at a time when he was poised to win the Korean war and simultaneously knock out Red China as a military power, anything which could be said for American anti-Communist policy over VOA would have sounded unreal.

Mr. Barrett learned painfully that a propaganda operation is valueless to a nation unless it is linked to a foreign policy which can be sold to the world. American foreign policy, in the days of Acheson and Jessup, couldn't even be sold to the American people.

Another thing which quickly bogged down the VOA program was the mischievous intrusion of petty domestic politics in the VOA efforts. The Voice script writers, guided by their policy chiefs, found themselves portraying to the world not the real America but an Acheson-Truman America. Since 1953 they have expediently switched to a noisy, 'round-the-clock and 'round-the-world presentation of an Eisenhower America.

Its timidity and indecision were exemplified by the Voice when it waited from June 25, 1950, to August 14, 1950, before broadcasting the fact that Russia was the aggressor nation in Korea. The seven weeks' delay enabled the Russians and the Chinese Communists to fix an entirely different stereotype in the Asian mind.

In June, 1951, when American and South Korean forces were holding a large area of North Korea above the 38th Parallel, the Voice again played directly into Russia's hands by broadcasting approvingly Trygve Lie's UN offer to arrange an armistice based on American withdrawal to the 38th Parallel. Needless to say this announcement was in direct contradiction of the policy of the American commander in Korea.

With even greater stupidity, while South Korean troops were fighting heroically beside Americans, the VOA was actually beaming broadcasts to South Korea sharply critical of President Syngman Rhee, the strongest anti-Communist figure in East Asia. VOA meddling in domestic Korean politics became so obnoxious to the South Koreans that Rhee's government was constrained to deny South Korean radio facilities to the Voice.

When General MacArthur, as Supreme Commander, sent his famous message to the Veterans of Foreign Wars in 1951 declaring that Formosa should not be allowed to fall into the hands of an unfriendly power, the VOA broadcast in 24 foreign languages that President Truman had ordered the General to withdraw his statement.

When General MacArthur was summarily fired from his Far East supreme command, the Voice beamed to the world a slanted pro-Truman version of the shabby performance.

Similar reluctance to discuss national news events objectively when they concern Administration figures was shown in the Voice handling of the Hiss case. When Whittaker Chambers' *Witness* was published, the head of the French desk in the Voice instructed a subordinate not to review it on the air, and expressed his opinion that Chambers was a psychopathic case.

On such an issue as the Katyn Forest murders, per-
petrated by the Russian troops during the war, the
Voice was afraid to use this crushingly effective propaganda argument against Moscow. When Count Joseph
Czapski, one of the few survivors of this horror, visited
the United States in 1950 and spoke over the Voice to
his countrymen, he was asked to omit all references to
Katyn in his speech, when he submitted his text in advance.

If the editorial policies of the Voice are weak and often pointless, its personnel is, for the most part, third-
rate. For an operation which has set itself to win the
mind of the world in competition with Communism,
the highest order of controversial brains is needed.
America has such brains, but they are not and never
have been in the VOA.

Instead, Benton, Allen, Barrett and finally Compton
and his successors gathered around themselves a dreary
company of uninspired script writers, with negligible
journalistic or radio experience. The most conspicuous
group among these were the dedicated internationalists
and Left Wingers.

There is something almost Gilbert-and-Sullivanlike in
the spectacle of the United States challenging international Communism to a world debate with such ap-
peasers, anti-anti-Communists, Socialists, political bus
boys and plain misguided individuals writing and speaking the American script.

The late Senator Robert A. Taft declared shortly before he died that if he had been in a position of power,
he "would have fired the whole Voice of America set-
up."

One misconception which is being encouraged today by our present bureaucrats in Washington is that the cost of VOA is all that Uncle Sam pays for radio. Pleaders for VOA appropriations before Congressional committees conveniently omit the fact that United States money goes to three other costly radio ventures, in addition to the USIA's Voice. The total Federal bill for radio is not just $18,000,000, the current VOA budgeted figure; actually it is nearer to $100,000,000. This huge sum, spent for radio only, means that terse, professionally presented factual news programs, beamed only to the behind-the-Iron-Curtain countries, often become a mere sideline and are lost in an avalanche of global gabble. If any foreign nation, friend or foe, attempted to clutter up our airways with anything approximating this overdose of "yackety-yack-yack," Americans would, very likely, shut off or destroy their radios.

Omitted in all Voice discussions is the fact that Armed Forces Radio Service, conducted by the Office of Information and Education of the Department of Defense, expends (including personnel overhead) approximately $50,000,000 to $60,000,000 a year. AFRS is a world-wide operation, sending from Hollywood some 10,000 radio transcriptions each week and reaching an estimated global public of 90,000,000 hearers, including all the English-speaking public in the areas where our armed forces are stationed. Without the fanfare and the boasting of VOA, AFRS makes a quiet, workmanlike effort to win public goodwill, as it has since 1942, when it made its bow.

Also omitted from the usual VOA debate is the fact that Radio Free Europe and Radio Free Asia, ostensibly private broadcasters, allegedly draw the major part of their $25,000,000 annual spendings from grants from the Federal Treasury. RFE and RFA particularize in broadcasts across the Iron Curtain by former Communists, and do a useful specialized work. But it must not be overlooked that they are a part of the *total* U. S. radio picture.

A third radio agency, financed by the United States separately from VOA, is Radio Station RIAS in Berlin, which is carried in the HICOG budget of the Department of State. In 1954 the United States allocated approximately $3,600,000 to this, the most widely heard of our radio propaganda vehicles.

The pretense that our government radio program is a relatively inexpensive $18,000,000 USIA proposition is a dishonest depictment of the actual situation. Americans must keep their eyes sighted on the $100,000,000 figure to keep their attitudes toward overly exploited VOA in proper perspective.

In both text and mechanical transmission, the quality of the Voice often is extremely poor. Unlike privately operated radio programs the Voice is supposed to enhance the prestige and name of the United States. However, it frequently misinterprets the beliefs and hopes of the majority of Americans. It often gives global publicity to speeches of Washington politicians, many of which are purely for home consumption and should not be broadcast, at public expense to foreigners whose goodwill and confidence we seek. Moreover, the Voice time and again exploits and magnifies purely American disputes and problems of strictly domestic concern.

Early in 1954, following an "H" bomb test in the Pacific, there occurred an accident to some Japanese fishermen. The Voice made a "stirring serial" out of the unfortunate incident together with premature comments of high Washington officials, made before proper investigations had been completed and reported. The project couldn't have been more unfortunately timed. It enabled our critics within the governments of Great Britain, France and other countries to condemn us officially in both their parliaments and their press.

Again, just before the ill-fated Geneva meeting, Secretary Dulles attempted to enlist the assurance of the governments of Great Britain and France that they would stand firm with us and form a solid front against the demands of Red China. The Voice revealed the plan before it had been received officially by the two European governments concerned.

But even were the Voice administered by imaginative and intellectually courageous men, it still would be incapable of doing the job which its admirers promise. The Voice is the prisoner of its own medium. We have oversold ourselves on our own gadget.

Actually, radio in its present status is not geared for a saturation coverage of the world population. Over broad areas of the world, radio reception is a luxury enjoyed only by the privileged few.

Let us consider the Iron Curtain countries, which are our prime target. In Russia itself only 4,000,000 sets are distributed among 211,000,000 people.

When we turn to Asia, the ratios become wider. Thus in India with a population of approximately 356,000,-

,ooo there are only 750,000 receivers, 516,000 capable of receiving our shortwave digests. Pakistan, with a population of 75,843,000, has only 56,500 shortwave receivers. Indonesia, with 79,260,000 people, has only 39,000.

Radio is not the easy answer to the propaganda problem. And if radio is still only effective in the Western world, television, which the Voice administrators are now talking about as their next medium, must be dismissed as years away.

But even if, by some sudden miraculous manna of receiving sets, the world's backwardness in radio reception were removed, the Voice would still face the insoluble obstacle of jamming.

The premise upon which the whole Voice program was projected—that the world's air lanes are open and give us an uninterruptible path into the minds of the enemy population—is only partially true. Russia's sensational jamming techniques, which have kept all except 20 to 30 per cent of our Voice programs out of Russia, demonstrate the sharp limitations on international broadcasting. Director Streibert, appearing before the National Press Club in Washington in July, 1954, confessed that *none* of our programs is getting through to Moscow.

Moscow is a city of six million people. It is the seat of government and the principal city of the Soviet Union. For five years the distinguished American reporter, Harrison E. Salisbury, represented the New York *Times* as its Chief Correspondent in the Soviet Union. When Mr. Salisbury returned to the United States, in the fall of 1954, this revealing comment, made by him, appeared in *Variety:*

"Salisbury, who was one of ten western newsmen covering from the Soviet capital, considers the 'Voice of America' broadcasts to Russia virtually useless, partly due to effective Russian jamming and partly because in areas *outside* Moscow, where American broadcasts do get through, the populace isn't much interested in any radio pitch from abroad. Salisbury said the radio short wave story was vastly different when it came to the Red satellites."

The fact remains that the Voice has failed miserably in its efforts to sell America. It has not made an important dent in the accumulation of ill-will from which America suffers so poignantly abroad. The Voice, in its nine post-war years, has shown sadly that it is not America's way of escape from the great national dilemma which confronts us. And measured in both friendships lost and dollars wasted, its maintenance cost is out of all proportion to its very small accomplishments.

A random sampling of VOA broadcasts gives a painful picture of its inadequacies.

Tens of thousands of passengers travelling to and from Europe on the Cunard liners listen to both the British Broadcasting Company (BBC) and the Voice of America programs. These are taped from the air by the vessel's wireless officer and carried through the ship's communications system to its lounges and smoking rooms. The BBC broadcast is usually given at 6 P.M. and the same program is repeated at 9 P.M. ship's time. This is immediately followed by the fifteen-minute English language overseas broadcast of the Voice of America, which is likewise repeated at 9:15 P.M.

Here are the notes of a listener who followed the

programs on the *Queen Elizabeth,* from March 31 to April 5, 1954.

Voice of America.

Broadcast of April 2.

Delivery entirely too fast for any European or non-American to absorb or understand.

Text of broadcast sounded like the product of a verbose young fellow palming off his first essay before a public speaking class at school.

Diction of the announcer poor, flat and harsh in contrast to the authoritative, measured and slow delivery of the BBC commentators who preceded the USIA broadcast.

Transmission full of flutters. BBC transmission was clear and crisp.

BBC's news was concise, its reports interesting and covering, in terse short sentences, a wide variety of British Empire news and sports.

The Voice program started with a bombast to exploit the Administration's ideas of McCarthy to the world. This was just before the Army-McCarthy hearings in Washington.

Following this opening news item a further mention of the controversial Senator from Wisconsin was made in reporting an anti-McCarthy resolution offered, and defeated, at a Republican State Convention in Maine.

All mention was omitted of the critical battle then raging in Indo-China, which was covered as a top news item in a terse report carried in the BBC broadcast that preceded the Voice.

The entire broadcast, and all others, carried over the loudspeakers of the *Queen Elizabeth* were inferior to the BBC news program that came ahead of the Voice, and often in-accurate.

A Texan who was a nightly listener remarked, after hearing both news programs on the night of April 2:

"We are promoting the latest ideas of the White House crowd instead of telling the news. I never ex-pected to have to listen to the British program to get an interesting and unbiased news report. Even their daily account of their cricket games sounds natural."

The Voice has failed, but it goes on—a permanent charge upon the defenseless American taxpayer. The Democrats under Truman have gone and the Republi-cans under Eisenhower have come, but with the ex-ception of a few new faces in the front office, the same VOA crowd that failed so utterly in the past is still manning the microphones.

The Appropriations Committees of the 83rd Congress patiently listened to the depressing story of VOA fail-ure, spelled out in chapter and verse, and then, in obe-dience to pressure from high quarters, it proceeded to vote approximately $18,000,000 more to continue the Voice for another futile year.

This is more than the deficit-ridden American peo-ple can afford to waste, especially when it is recalled that the Voice actually is only one fifth of America's hundred-million-dollar-a-year bill for radio propaganda overseas! But like the Merovingian Kings we may ex-pect to see the VOA go on and on, although any social usefulness it may have had under the excitement of war time has long since vanished in the era of the Cold War.

But, as we shall see, the VOA is only a part of the

shabby and shameful chronicle of great waste which is being written by the vaunted United States Information Agency. Now let's look at Uncle Sam's movies that have cost Americans tens of millions of dollars—movies you will *never* see!

8

Uncle Sam's Movie Madness

If Uncle Sam ever should make up his mind to apply the meat-axe to some of the encrusted barnacles which cling to the United States Information Agency, he would not have to search far for a target.

A logical starting point would be the International Motion Picture Service, which has plunged Uncle Sam headlong into the movie business, producing propaganda films for use abroad.

Of all the follies put over on an unsuspecting public by our self-styled psychological warriors, this flicker nonsense is perhaps the most costly and indefensible.

Few Hollywood producers of stature would ever take any personal responsibility for the kind of film nonsense we have been shipping abroad for years in the vain hope that by this means we can combat Soviet-inspired propaganda.

Anyone with even scant understanding of the minds of our Allies realizes that any motion picture which even faintly hints of propaganda will never be accepted by them. Neither will it contribute to the downfall of Communism. Europeans particularly have been exposed to propaganda since the days of Hitler and Mussolini. They have developed an immunity to it that probably will never wear off.

This basic political reality is recognized by Eric Johnston, president of the Motion Picture Association of America. Returning from Europe several years ago, Mr. Johnston advised Hollywood:

"If we deliberately made propaganda films, our industry would not only go bust, but would be doing the worst possible service for America."

It's highly unfortunate, almost tragic, that this sage advice has not been noted or followed in Washington.

Few Americans have any idea how deeply involved the U. S. has become in the making of propaganda films which, in Eric Johnston's words, are "doing the worst possible service for America."

Already we have amassed more than 1,000 subjects and 70,000 prints of one- and two-reel Government-produced documentaries. These are rotated out to field missions throughout the world with little regard for local needs. Thus, generally speaking, information centers in Norway, Siam, Iran, or Korea are provided with the same films. The "One Worlders," who mold the policies of U. S. overseas propaganda, plan production of films on a global basis.

As John C. Caldwell, a former U. S. Information officer, pointed out in his book, *The Korea Story*, USIA geniuses in Washington appear to operate on the assumption that the Icelander thinks and acts the same way as the Zulu, the Portuguese and the Mongolian.

Films on low-cost housing, Mr. Caldwell pointed out, "showing the Peter Stuyvesant Village project in lower Manhattan, simply cannot be of help to Koreans, struggling with mud and straw to solve their own housing problem."

Once, when Mr. Caldwell requested Washington to send a film on typical American college life, he received a documentary about UCLA, one of our largest and best-equipped universities.

"We had to show it to Korean students who studied all winter in barnlike, unheated buildings with no textbooks, no laboratory equipment," he reported.

It goes without saying, of course, that Americans produce the finest documentaries in the world. But these visual instruction media, traditionally financed by educational groups and foundations, are created strictly for American scholastic audiences.

What the bright boys at USIA are doing is making films for overseas use based on American know-how, alien to the thinking of most foreigners.

As Mr. Caldwell so well put it:

"These films present an advanced technology hardly within the dream, much less the practical reach, of a large percentage of the world's population. Koreans happen to be a polite people and they did not often point this out. The Communists did it for them."

To date, about $100,000,000 has been poured down the government's movie-making drainpipe. Uncle Sam has purchased some 6,700 sound projectors, each costing about $400, and a fleet of 355 mobile film units, costing over $6,000 each. Total investment in equipment alone exceeds $5,000,000.

It was during the try-anything OWI war days that Uncle Sam got into movie production in a big way.

Although no convincing reason for the continuance of an official U. S. motion picture agency has ever been adduced by its defenders, the program grinds on, like so many other obsolete Government agencies, carried forward by the sheer momentum of its activities and its global personnel.

As the foreign aid agencies burgeoned up—Point Four and Technical Assistance, Mutual Security Administration, etc.—each in turn developed its own film agencies with which to promote and perpetuate its programs.

Uncle Sam, by now, not only found himself neck-deep in the film business, he began to be choked.

However, let's concentrate on what USIA's film division has been doing. What kind of films have they been making?

For the most part, previous efforts have been of a documentary, travelogue type. They have carried such titles as "Paper Tiger," "Screw Worms," "Grasshoppers," "Bees a-Buzzing," "Anna's Hummingbird," "Sweeney Steps Out," "Music for Tiny Tots," "Fulton Fish Market," "The Ancient Curse," "Highway to Hawaii," and "Christmas in Vermont." The USIA's promoters, according to *Variety*, claim that "Christmas in

Vermont" proved popular because it showed lots of snow to people who have never encountered it in their own experiences.

How "lots of snow" can sell peoples abroad on the necessity of combatting Communism is something which was not explained.

One Motion Picture Service catalogue, listing USIA films available in Germany, gives such gems of American self-portraiture as, "Window Washing in the Empire State Building," "Children's Zoo at Bronx Park," "New York's Sailor's Home," "Sunday in New York," and "Camping for Girl Scouts."

Perhaps one of the frankest comments upon the quality of these films was made by J. Cheever Cowdin, a former Wall Street investment banker and theatrical film company chairman, whom Dr. Robert L. Johnson brought briefly to Washington to head up the film program during his own four months as USIA director. Cowdin told the House Appropriations Committee that "our [film] libraries abroad are perfectly pathetic."

Mr. Cowdin's solution, unfortunately, was to spend more money on new films.

Who sees these films?

"It is mostly the people who do not go to motion picture theaters that will see these pictures," Dr. Johnson told the House Committee.

"How will they see them?" asked Representative Frederic R. Coudert (Rep., N.Y.).

"We have little trucks, some 300 of them, that will take these pictures out into villages, way back in the country, where many of the people cannot read, and where they do not even have newspapers."

Most of these people, it would be safe to say, are more in need of something to eat than a movie showing how the Empire State Building's windows are washed.

Moreover, instead of making Free World converts we have at times provided ready-made audiences for Communist propagandists. Typical was an incident in a rural community in southern France.

A USIA mobile film truck stopped near a road juncture near the town. It blared a recording of a popular and familiar American band number, until a crowd collected. Then followed the pièce de résistance—a documentary film showing the wealthy and thrifty French farmers how to till their soil better! *Only* our propagandists are unaware that the soil of French farms is the most productive on earth!

Even before *fin* was flashed on the screen, the truck was set to take off. The dust had hardly settled before a local Communist agitator took over the audience provided for him with this cooperation of USIA. The agitator, more familiar with his community's problems and weaknesses than all of the U. S. propagandists put together, launched a noisy tirade about "the Wall Street warmongers who give you cinemas and circuses instead of bread." And grisly French farmers nodded vigorous approval!

Multiply the incident a thousandfold in France, in Italy and elsewhere, and you can gain an idea of the continuing harmfulness of USIA shenanigans abroad. No wonder, then, we are continuing to lose our friends overseas on a wholesale scale.

No other country on earth engages continually in this kind of flicker foolishness; certainly not the Soviet

Union whose followers are always around to ridicule and condemn it.

It might be asked, How would Americans feel if the situation were reversed and some foreign nation should clutter up our highways with trucks showing their inappropriate and tiresome propaganda films created to exploit a way of life and a foreign scene that would prove uninteresting and offensive to the overwhelming majority of Americans?

Most Americans, if they had any sense of pride left, would deeply resent it. And, as Americans, they'd make their resentment known.

Yet, that's exactly what we intend to continue doing in the seemingly never-ending USIA campaign to remold the thinking of foreigners to our liking.

A revealing example of the impact of USIA's propaganda short films on foreign viewers was unconsciously given by Edward Purcell, Public Relations Officer for the USIA in the State of Rio Grande do Sul, Brazil.

Mr. Purcell, while on vacation at home, was honored by the Agency with a special interview on Brazilian political conditions, all widely publicized in a USIA press handout. The Public Relations Officer drew a favorable picture of American propaganda work in Brazil, and he praised his Agency's motion picture program. "Children are brought in by bus from rural schools to see the pictures and love them. Community officials give us every cooperation," Mr. Purcell said, and he added, "Cartoon films are particularly popular." He referred to one, the story of the chicken city terrorized by the big Red Fox. "The audience gets the point," he added.

But, in the very same release, Mr. Purcell unhappily

refutes his own optimism and indicates that kiddie cartoons and movie showings in remote jungle places are hardly enough to discourage Communist growth in Brazil:

"Communist activities in Latin America are definitely on the increase," said Mr. Purcell. "I have seen the [Communist] campaign developing over a period of three years. But recently it has been very definitely stepped up. As I see it the fight in Latin America has just begun."

When the Republican Administration took office, Uncle Sam had an excellent opportunity to get rid of the USIA's useless and often harmful motion picture service.

The new Administration had promised unsparing economy in Federal expenditures. What better place was there to institute drastic budget slashes than in the admittedly inept USIA and its film activities?

Two possible courses of action confronted the new government heads. Either the motion picture service could have been eliminated entirely with no weakening at all of the over-all information program. Or else, it could have been drastically reduced. Now, the Service was already equipped with a sufficient stock of educational films which could have supplied the normal requirements of educational exhibitors abroad for a period of ten years or longer, without any new production, if the second course had been followed.

Unfortunately, neither course was taken. Instead the new Administration advocated an astounding increase in the budget for the motion picture service! The USIA had sold a bill of goods to the White House!

When President Eisenhower's budget recommendations were disclosed, the motion picture extravaganza
was down for nearly $7,000,000—almost double the
1953-54 Truman grant. The newly appointed film director went before the House Appropriations Committee to declare that $12,000,000 for propaganda films
was nearer the amount wanted!

Fortunately there still were some patriots left in
Congress with concern for the public purse. The Appropriations Committee of the House flatly refused
to be taken in by the ambitious scheme of the USIA's
top spokesmen.

They saw to it that the motion picture service was
granted $3,390,117. However, in fiscal 1955, the figure
was actually raised more than half a million dollars by
the chief spokesmen for the Senate Appropriations Committee, despite the vigorous objection of their counter-
parts in the House Appropriations Committee.

This action was all the more indefensible in view of
the fact that the United States is the one nation in the
world which needs no movie propaganda abroad. This
is so because our Hollywood-made entertainment films
have dominated the movie theaters of the world for half
a century.

Some 200,000,000 foreigners see our theatrical films
weekly because they are entertainment, completely
free of propaganda. These films show Americans as they
really are, for better or worse. Though they carry no
messages, they offer a weary world solid entertainment,
and show how a free people lives and laughs.

The "tremendous impact of American entertainment
motion pictures have on all people abroad, particularly

those behind the Iron Curtain," has been reported by Irving Brown, the American Federation of Labor's European representative.

"American motion pictures are popular primarily because of their superior entertainment value," Brown declared. "People the world over are weary of the type of propaganda fed them every day by Communists.

"Even though American motion pictures are seen because of their entertainment value, they carry social and ideological by-products because through the movies people of other countries form their ideas, impressions and prejudices of the American way of life.

"It is because American films have no conscious propaganda that they have a powerful influence abroad. This is true whether the movie is 'good' or 'bad.' "

The testimonials to the effectiveness of Hollywood entertainment films in selling friendship for America abroad are profuse.

"American motion pictures have provided more pleasure for more people than any other agency in the world," declared Sir Roger Makins, the British Ambassador to the United States.

"Your movies are your best ambassadors," declared one of Italy's top newspaper editors, Massimi Olmi, of Rome's *Il Momento,* while touring the United States.

American motion pictures have spread tolerance and understanding among peoples of the world, according to Dag Hammarskjold, United Nations Secretary-General. He said: "The American motion picture has had much to do with the fact that through a large part of the world when somebody has an inclination to bang his neighbor on the head, he stops and thinks twice before doing it."

According to *The Film Daily,* the Indonesian Minister for Religious Affairs had this to say: "American films, featuring music, dancing, light drama, religion and comedy situations attract the largest audiences in our theaters. These pictures, devoid of any form of propaganda, are most popular because of their entertainment values which, in turn, develop goodwill between the two countries."

Mahmud Shafqat, first Secretary of the Pakistan Embassy in Washington, declared that Hollywood pictures have contributed greatly in preparing the world to accept the leadership of the United States in international affairs. Addressing a Hollywood luncheon, the diplomat declared that "the American public does not fully realize the importance of movies as unofficial ambassadors of goodwill."

When certain key legislators began asking embarrassing questions concerning the value of U. S. propaganda pictures, the USIA headed for Hollywood for help.

Cecil B. De Mille, one of Hollywood's veteran spectacle film makers, was appointed to the hastily conceived post of "honorary" film consultant.

Mr. De Mille obtained a lot of personal publicity and the constant use of his name helped to bolster the sagging USIA movie effort, but as a "consultant" he was not too helpful. De Mille came up with the amazing conclusion that the real trouble with the USIA was that it didn't spend enough money on movies!

In a much quoted telegram to the then USIA Di-

bert L. Johnson, Mr. De Mille assailed
ness of U. S. propaganda films and rec-
hat hereafter they be made Hollywood-
ne idea of what he meant was his statement
his own next film would cost more than four million dollars.

He implied that no effective propaganda film could
be created for less than the cost of a good quality Hollywood production. Such pictures might cost as much as
$2,000,000 each. Since the USIA was then making
about fifty documentary films annually, Mr. De Mille's
program could involve a yearly expenditure for film
production *alone* of about $100,000,000. This sum
would be $25,000,000 more than the entire 1953-54
budget of $75,000,000 for all of the Government's
global propaganda extravagances.

Even Dr. Johnson's successor as USIA director
gagged on this ambitious idea. At a Washington press
conference, Mr. Streibert denied that the USIA was
considering production of propaganda films on the
super-Hollywood scale advocated by Mr. De Mille. He
stated flatly that the Government could not afford
Hollywood's production costs for its new propaganda
films.

Another incredible statement contained in the De
Mille telegram was his reference to the "hopeless and
perhaps useless" battle the U. S. was waging against
Communist film propaganda. He asserted that Soviet
films he had seen were "brilliantly made and costly,"
adding that "I have not seen anything made by our
motion picture service comparable in power."

One can only wonder what "brilliantly made" Soviet films Mr. De Mille could have been referring to.

An earlier Senate report on Soviet propaganda pointed out that the Kremlin operates at a great disadvantage compared to the United States since "the Soviet film industry is relatively underdeveloped." In the United States the annual output of feature-length films amounts to about 350, and the majority of these are shown abroad. Soviet Union features that are exported for showing to foreign audiences average about 12 per annum.

For still further proof of the effectiveness of Hollywood films as compared with those turned out under strict Kremlin direction let us turn to Berlin, where the East Zone Germans are not sufficiently hemmed in by the Iron Curtain to be kept entirely away from the outside world.

The Los Angeles *Times,* in a dispatch from Berlin, reported that East Germans were flocking to West Zone theaters, where the charms of such as Marilyn Monroe could be seen on display.

"[According to the dispatch] So great is the Communist officials' embarrassment at empty movie houses in East Berlin, that they give away tickets and even march workers from the factory to movie 'recreation.'

"Meanwhile, in West Berlin movie theaters, East Germans—who eight years after the end of the war are still going hungry—enjoy Hollywood movies which portray life that is worth living, showing people free to be happy and to enjoy themselves. They get a pretty good idea of what they are to believe of Russian propaganda which tries to depict the 'capitalist' United States as a country where 'workers are held down in extreme poverty.'

"As my Soviet-zone friends explained it to me on their regular visits to free Berlin: 'No advertising could do a better job. If the Communists attack something as furiously as they do American movies, it simply means that Hollywood is doing a good job.'

"To understand their craving one has to realize that they can choose only between East German film products or Russian movies. They hate both.

"From seeing these films the East Germans learn that the Soviets' ideal is work, work, work. A life of drudgery in drab clothes without any interests beyond those of the ever-powerful Communist state.

"For in a Communist state movies are neither entertainment nor escape and they are not intended to be."

Even behind the Iron Curtain, when an occasional American film is shown, it still outdraws Red products. An American traveler reported that while he was in Czechoslovakia he would "have to wait for as many as five weeks to see an American film, when I could have had a theater showing Russian pictures practically to myself."

Eric Johnston reported a similar experience. He saw "long lines waiting to get into already jam-packed theaters showing American films. In contrast, Soviet films were unwinding to almost empty seats."

Why do American films, even "bad" ones, outdraw the Soviets' "brilliantly made and costly" pictures?

The reason, of course, is that they are free of propaganda.

Another error Mr. De Mille has attempted to convey

is the unsupported claim that USIA propaganda films are reaching an audience of 500 million people a year "at a cost of a little over one cent per contact."

Mr. De Mille, who would never run his own affairs on the basis of press-agented claims, has thus accepted a bit of oft-repeated and fraudulent USIA press-agentry, which unfortunately also was taken as Gospel by such Senators as Iowa's Bourke Hickenlooper, whose long legislative experience should have made him more wary.

No proof for these audience figures, which were trotted out regularly for several years at appropriation time, has ever been given. The fact is that it is a virtual impossibility to obtain this kind of global audience, even if the coverage made were intensive and honestly accounted for, which it was not.

On one of his many trips abroad, the writer asked a USIA official to estimate how many French farmers viewed a short film on the use of American tractors. The official said it was impossible to make even a guess. He did say that individual audiences could not have consisted of more than ten to twenty-five people, since, because of the specialized subject matter, the film's use was limited.

Yet, the head of the section reported to Washington that the tractor film was seen by an audience in excess of 100,000 in France alone!

Probably the most sweeping indictment of the futility of the USIA's American taxpayer supported propaganda movies for foreigners vs. the universal acceptance and effectiveness of Hollywood's *non*-propaganda films came from the New York *Times* reporter Harrison E.

Salisbury. As previously noted in these pages, Mr. Salisbury spent five years in the Soviet Union. *Variety* reported his comments on American movies in Russia:

"The *Times* scribe who's travelled all over the Soviet Union said Russian audiences are fascinated by the detail in American films. Hollywood pictures, almost regardless of their quality or content, are big ads for the United States," he opined. "The mere fact that we can make films without propaganda content is in our favor and always a matter of comment. There is no question that in Russia, as everywhere else, American pictures are the best and most forceful medium for selling the U.S. It's a shame we're not availing ourselves of that opportunity."

(Mr. Salisbury strongly advocates selling the Soviet Union more Hollywood non-propaganda entertainment films. Presently the Russians are restricted to showing mostly old pictures captured as "war booty.")

And, *even in the Soviet,* propaganda movies, made by the Russians, are a failure!

"Salisbury reported that Russian features tended not to be very good or very popular, but that the government has now instituted a new line which sees the content of the pictures are pitched *more toward entertainment and less toward propaganda.* Ironically, he observed, Russian producers aren't sure what to make of this new freedom!"

Hollywood appears to have recognized the dangers inherent in our propaganda films, particularly of the type advocated by Mr. De Mille. For the kind of films he wants the USIA to produce must, of necessity, compete with products of our own entertainment industry, since they can only reach large enough audiences to justify their production costs through intensive exhibition on the theater screens of foreign countries.

The true American story is a saga of heart-stirring content. Properly told, as the entertainment film producers have consistently done it, the American story has gripped the imagination of the world. But the USIA is not telling that story.

Instead it is engaging in all sorts of questionable borderline undertakings designed to trick foreign audiences into seeing and hearing outright American propaganda. In disregard of all movie industry experience, it is making, and intends to continue making, costly foreign propaganda films in foreign countries in the hope that they can be shown on a "sneak" basis in foreign commercial movie houses. In Italy, Austria and the Far East it is attempting to subsidize foreign newsreels. It squanders tens of thousands of dollars to photograph and record in a dozen languages such goodwill tours as that of Vice President Nixon in the Orient (including a now totally inappropriate Indo-China sequence) and the visit of Dr. Milton S. Eisenhower to South America, despite the fact that all news interest in these tours has passed long before they can be exhibited.

And now, still determined to perpetuate its international film service with its costly worldwide "film officer" personnel, together with its distributing officers, projector operators and plush little theaters, the USIA film promoters have hit upon a thrilling new scheme to keep the Washington legislators from asking questions at appropriation time.

They are now embarked upon a "top secret" program of producing "cloak and dagger" propaganda films with dialogue and casts of little known Hollywood actors. The first of these was completed in a West Coast studio, its title, "Poles Are Stubborn People." This blood and thunder flicker was quickly followed by another Hollywood produced movie under the cheerful title "Rape of the Baltic." Additionally, the USIA boasts of an atrocity film issued under the happy title of "An Unpleasant Subject," a documentary on atrocities committed against United Nations troops in Korea by Chinese and North Korean Communists.

Another celluloid irritant that the USIA is attempting to ease into foreign theaters where people pay to be entertained is entitled "Dance of Freedom." This outright propaganda film is offered as USIA's newest conception of "The American Story," and it baldly portrays the dangers of Communism by the plight of two famous Hungarian dancers who flee from behind the Iron Curtain to freedom in West Berlin. This artistic "nifty," complete with dancing, will no doubt cause the Comrades in Moscow to shiver and shake!

These films are exactly the kind of "inspired" propaganda melodramas that Americans would seriously condemn if the men in the Kremlin attempted to impose them on foreign audiences. They are the kind of films whose production Eric Johnston has warned "would be doing the worst possible service for America."

More recently, Mr. Chester Bahn, editor of the *New York Film Daily*, stated:

"Putting it baldly, this identification of Government films with American distribution easily could cast suspicion upon the entertainment product which comes out of Hollywood. . . . Let such product be tied too closely to USIA films and we provide the Commies with still another potent weapon for use in the fight against both Hollywood and the United States. . . . We complain . . . and surely with justification . . . that the Soviets load their pictures with propaganda and employ them abroad as so many instruments of government policy . . . should we give the Reds an excuse for countering with, 'Look, who's talking' . . . we certainly should not! ! !"

And all Americans are paying the bill of tens of millions of dollars for this "worst possible service for America." Meanwhile, the ambitious propaganda agency promoters issue fraudulent statements and global exhibition reports to the authoritative Associated and United Press services, and continue to seek new, more expensive and more harmful methods to justify and perpetuate this movie madness.

9

The USIA Talks About Itself

US information Agency

For the first time in the peacetime history of the United States, the American people are being treated to the spectacle of a Federal agency spending nearly a quarter of a million dollars a year to tell us how good it is.

Other Government organizations, of comparable scope, find it sufficient to employ a competent press liaison officer to supply the information needs of the press. The United States Information Agency employs fifteen executives to handle its selling program to the American home public. Their output consists of over-clever articles about the Soviet menace as the USIA sees it, and unblushing press-agentry of USIA accomplishments.

The unsuspecting American taxpayer is footing the bill for a high-pressure drive to persuade him to appropriate more money for the high-pressurers. This is certainly propaganda in reverse.

We were given a clear picture of this home program on February 2, 1954, when Mr. Theodore C. Streibert, USIA Director, appeared before the subcommittee of the Committee on Appropriations of the House of Representatives to urge an appropriation of $89 million for his agency.

It was Mr. John J. Rooney, Democratic Congressman from Brooklyn, who surprised the hearings by questioning the need for so much money for the obvious. Mr. Rooney was never known as a serious opponent of the propaganda agency's requests, hence his critical stand was the more startling. From the record:

MR. ROONEY: I notice that you have in this budget $204,-639 which appears under "Congressional and Public Information Staff." Do we need to spend $204,000 of the taxpayers' money to tell the American people what, *if anything,* you are doing, and to maintain liaison with Capitol Hill?

MR. STREIBERT: Printing and reproduction accounts for $110,000 of that for 1955.

MR. ROONEY: And personal services $98,000 and travel $6,000?

MR. STREIBERT: Well that is for fifteen people.

MR. ROONEY: Could we not very well do away with this little item?

MR. STREIBERT: I think it ought to be about five times what it is, sir, and I will tell you why:

There has been more criticism of this information service than almost any other branch of the Government. It is highly controversial, and it is largely a matter of opinion.

The public has heard in the past primarily the criticisms. This agency has never attempted to tell the taxpayers what is happening to their money.

MR. ROONEY: Well that is all very well and nice, but what about the taxpayers having to pay over $200,000 for such?

MR. STREIBERT: I think they have a right, sir, to have information at least available to them—without any *high-pressure* public relations campaign—but at least they should have the means of knowing how this money is being spent, and that is one of the main purposes of this item. . . . I find a great ignorance on the part of the public and I am sure you do too.

MR. ROONEY: No; I have been reading some delightful press releases from this agency which have been coming across my desk for the past many, many months making statements that you are doing this and that, all of which we heard years ago. . . .

MR. STREIBERT: Some people do not know what libraries are.

MR. ROONEY: Is that important? Suppose they don't. I have always thought that we were spending money in order to pierce the Iron Curtain, and to keep our relations elsewhere in the world in good shape.

I did not think we were spending money to barrage the American people about what an alleged fine agency the Information Service is.

MR. STREIBERT: They have heard of these library criticisms and they really do not understand.

MR. ROONEY: *Never in the balmy days of the New Deal did they attempt such a thing as this.*

So important did the USIA regard this domestic activity that it threw in its heavy guns as the sessions of the appropriations committees dealing with the USIA

(*Above*). Uncle Sam paid Baron Rothschild a million dollars for this palace in Paris—in all the world no press agent's office like this!

Inner courtyard of this paradise for USIA press agents!

The Chateau Rothschild in Paris, now tenanted entirely by U. S. Information Agency press agents! It is as large as the British Embassy.

Another Paris headquarters for USIA press agents is the block-long and once-famed Café des Ambassadeurs, facing the garden of the Champs Élysées.

The USIA Library is the formerHotelAstoria,located in an ultrafashionable section of Paris—not convenient for French working masses.

Thousands of government payrollers require homes. Here is part of a new U. S. Government-furnished apartment project for "Yanks who won't go home." At 21-23c Quai du Septembre, Paris. Cost $5,000,000.

In Paris' swank Neuilly district another apartment building for government Yanks is being built by Uncle Sam. Wealthy French neighbors call these "Ike's Eyesores."

Rome. When U. S. Ambassadors in the Eternal City dealt *only* in diplomacy this edifice sufficed. Now it is a mere Consul's office!

The transition from our dignified Embassy of yesteryear to the extravagant colossus of today is through this formal Roman garden.

The former home of the Italian Queen Mother is now the U. S. Embassy in Rome. No other nation boasts of a palace like this—it is almost as large as London's Buckingham Palace!

Across from the main Embassy on the Via Vittoria Veneto are two seven-story hotel buildings now tenanted entirely by the Foreign Operations Administration and the United States Information Agency.

Once a royal Italian garden, complete with priceless statuary, now a parking lot for the USIA in Rome.

Our airmen bombed Rome during World War II. Now USIA propagandists pierce the peaceful Roman skies to promote "Atomic Bombs for Peace" —and to give the Communists ammunition to remind Romans of yesteryear!

Photo by James Whitmore

For a nation that symbolizes Democracy this great wall protecting the residence of the U. S. Ambassador to Italy is hardly appropriate . . . and beyond the wall *(right)*—this elaborate formal garden provides a regal setting for the U. S. Ambassador's residence.

At the heart of this kingly splendor resides the representative of our democracy—the U. S. Ambassador to Italy.

Our new million-dollar Embassy and cultural plant in Copenhagen confounds Danes, who predict it will not withstand the rigors of their winters.

Unlike the U.S.A., the British conform strictly to the climate of Denmark.

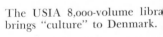

The USIA 8,000-volume library brings "culture" to Denmark.

And for the U.S.A.'s propaganda movie extravagance, a miniature theater.

The British have succeeded in maintaining good relations with this modest library and no movie theater.

Most South and Central Americans are very poor and envious of rich Uncle Sam. This pretentious U. S. Embassy in Rio de Janeiro, Brazil, perpetuates this envy.

In Havana, our friendly neighbors in little Cuba see this overstaffed and extravagant example of Uncle Sam's bureaucracy.

This fine Spanish mansion for years proved adequate while we were cool to Franco's government.

Now that we are giving Franco hundreds of millions of dollars, we must have this "new look" for U. S. diplomacy, culture, and propaganda in Madrid.

budget neared voting day. A press release of February
25 indicated this.

"Press Release No. 36. Sidney H. Fine, veteran newspaperman and Government information officer in Europe for
many years, has been transferred from Paris to the Washington headquarters of the U. S. Information Agency as
Chief of the Public Information Staff. . . . He will be responsible for the domestic information program. During
the last five and a half years, Mr. Fine was chief press relations officer in Europe, recently under Ambassador John C.
Hughes. . . . He served in London from 1942 to '44 as
FCC field correspondent. Mr. Fine was assigned to the embassy in Moscow, representing the Office of War Information from 1945 to '46. Returning from Moscow he was made
regional information officer for the Department of Commerce in Kansas City, Mo. He left the Commerce Department to go to Paris for the ECA. . . ."

"Burnett Anderson has been assigned to head the information Agency's domestic press section. He was previously
press officer for the Mutual Security Agency in Bonn, Germany. . . ."

It would be supposed that a commander would leave
his best generals in the field. The Director of the USIA
evidently concluded that the two experts, trained in
Paris, London, Moscow and Bonn, could serve the
USIA better doing a home-front selling job.

Other appointments to the home propaganda task
followed, each accompanied by a one- or two-page release describing the history and qualifications of the appointee. One of the most interesting of these was that
of Raymond R. Dickey, appointed as General Counsel

to the Agency. *Press Release No. 77* of May 4 describes Mr. Dickey's qualifications and functions, in part, as follows:

"Mr. Dickey has already materially assisted us during the last few months. His extensive legal and governmental experience, here and abroad, qualify [*sic*] him admirably for the position of general counsel. Mr. Dickey will be responsible for liaison between the U. S. Information Agency and Congress as well as for the Agency's legal affairs."

What legal chores Mr. Dickey performs in his counselor role is conjectural. But there can be little question of his all-round fitness for the high-class lobbying assignment which, in USIA language, is semantically described as "liaison."

The best picture of the home indoctrination job which the USIA is attempting may be gotten from the utterances of the top USIA spokesmen. The most voluble of these is Director Theodore S. Streibert himself.

One of the Streibert speeches was before the American Society of Newspaper Editors in Washington, April 16, 1954 (*Press Release No. 65*, five pages single-spaced). He said:

"The United States is in the international information field out of sheer necessity . . . it has been forced on us by the imperialistic ambitions of Soviet Communism. . . . We can't do it *by words alone*. President Eisenhower outlined the strategy for us when he said: The service must clearly and factually present to the world the policies and objectives of the United States. It is not enough for us to have sound policies dedicated to the goals of universal peace, freedom and progress. Those policies must be made known to and understood by all the people throughout the world. That is the policy of the U. S. Information Agency."

The Agency head himself is a case exhibit of the non-words-alone policy. In a three-month period of his directorship the USIA sent out ten releases, each averaging ten pages, single-spaced, of speeches made by Mr. Streibert himself. Apparently it is important whose "words" are meant.

Another word in this speech is "factually." Was the propaganda director serious in repeating this Eisenhower promise? Within six days after this high-minded speech, the USIA itself was guilty of one of the most unfactual breaches of the truth in recent news reporting. USIA *Press Release No. 69* announced that:

" 'A sharp increase in pro-Communist motion pictures is taking place in Southeast Asia,' Theodore C. Streibert said today. 'Movies with anti-Western and pro-Communist themes are being produced in the Chinese language and distributed in growing numbers throughout the Far East. In addition, Russian-made films with Chinese sub-titles are being shown increasingly to movie audiences in the countries of South East Asia. In Hong Kong alone, which is now the third largest film production center in the world, several hundred Chinese-language films are being turned out each year by pro-Communist producers. Russian films are also finding an interesting audience. . . . Throughout Southeast Asia, both the Chinese and the Russian-made films with Chinese sub-titles are making heavy inroads on pictures made by the West.' "

The truthfulness of this press release was almost immediately contradicted in the New York *Times*. On

May 11, 1954, the *Times* published the following news story:

FILM CENSOR DENIES U. S. CHARGE

"Singapore, May 10: Mrs. C. Koek, Singapore's official film censor, denied today an allegation made recently in Washington by the United States Information Agency that Communist films produced in the Far East were on the increase and were being shown in the main theatres of Hong Kong and Singapore. She said no Communist or anti-American film had been shown in Singapore since the Malayan emergency began six years ago."

The *Times* dispatch was immediately followed by one from the Far Eastern news director for the *New York Film Daily,* industry-wide trade publication. In a cable from Tokyo, the truth of the USIA release, which was carried by the leading press associations, was vigorously denied.

On another occasion Mr. Streibert said, "We have chosen to stick by facts—hard facts, not hard words." (*Bulletin No. 44,* 11 pages, single-spaced).

The aim is admirable, but only too frequently USIA falls so far short of it that it allows factual contradictions to appear in two portions of the same release. Take, for instance, the speech delivered by the Director to the General Session of the Institute for Education by Radio and Television (*Press Release No. 57,* dated April 5, 12 single-spaced pages):

"In tackling the job, the USIA employs a variety of approaches—wireless news service, pamphlets and posters, radio, motion pictures, overseas information centers stocked with books, and personal contacts. . . . Among these approaches, radio plays a unique role. . . . And it is the only *medium* [italics ours] which can penetrate the Iron Curtain. That's why three-fourths of the Voice of America programs are beamed to the Soviet Orbit."

A few paragraphs farther down in the speech the speaker said:

"The problem of getting facts around the world is a complex one. Consider the task of penetrating the Iron Curtain. . . . the task of overcoming Soviet efforts to prevent our broadcasts from being heard. One means they employ is jamming. It is estimated that the Soviets have in use as many as one thousand jamming stations located at some twenty-five major centers. It is further estimated that they spend more to destroy our signals than we spend on our entire world-wide broadcasting system."

And Mr. Streibert went on to say:

"Obviously they hear only what the Communists want them to hear."

Which paragraph is the public supposed to believe? In this same speech the Director said:

"When television comes into large scale use behind the Iron Curtain, the Kremlin will have in its hands a powerful and near-perfect medium of controlled thought. *No outside telecast will be able to get its signal in to compete with the picture as the Soviets portray it.* Thus, Western technology has put into the hands of the Soviet another method of keeping its people in subjection."

Two months earlier the Director's own press agents issued a release in support of the Agency's Ninth Annual report to Congress:

"Item No. 13—That provisions be made to develop a plan to utilize the powerful medium of television in the program."

In his speech of April 16 to the newspaper editors the Director announced: "My first responsibility was to organize the new Agency. . . . The Agency today is manned by skilled, professional trained people who know their jobs. . . . To supervise operations in the field we have appointed four traveling vice-presidents—we call them assistant area directors. There is one for each region of the world. They have authority to act for me and make decisions on the spot . . . they also keep the field force working and on the ball."

A one-page *Press Release, No. 78,* May 13, states:

"Theodore C. Streibert will leave New York today for a one month's inspection tour of the Agency's Far Eastern posts.

"The complete itinerary is as follows: London, Calcutta, Rangoon, Bangkok, Djakarta, Singapore, Colombo, Madras, Bombay, New Delhi, Karachi, New York."

Why was it necessary for the Director himself to do all this traveling after he had put the four vice-presidents "on the ball" to make the decisions "on the spot?"

On July 9, *Press Release No. 98,* in another detailed page account of departures, said:

"Theodore C. Streibert will leave New York Friday for London where he will begin a month's review of Agency's European operations. He will be accompanied by Mrs. Streibert. The itinerary follows: London, July 9-12; Paris, July 12-25; Amsterdam, July 25-26; Brussels, July 26-27; Bonn, July 27-Aug. 1; Berlin, Aug. 1-3; Munich, Aug. 3-4; Vienna, Aug. 4-7; New York, Aug. 8."

The USIA pulled out all stops in its attempted coverage of the hapless Geneva Conference in April, 1954. Director Streibert, although innocent of any journalistic experience, made it a point to head the USIA delegation to Geneva. This was followed by a general release, No. 68.

"The U. S. Government's overseas information activity will be stepped up to give special and detailed coverage to the Korean Political Conference, opening in Geneva on April 26, the U. S. Information Agency said today.

"Prompt and extensive reporting of what is happening at Geneva will be carried to all parts of the world by the Agency's press, radio and motion picture services.

"The Voice of America, for example, will step up its programs to the Far East from $8\frac{1}{4}$ to $10\frac{1}{4}$ hours daily, for the duration of the Conference. The two additional hours will be devoted primarily to the latest news from Geneva.

"Field officers of the Agency all over the world have been furnished extensive background material which will assist them in interpreting developments at the Conference.

"The U. S. Information Agency will be officially represented on the U. S. Delegation to the Geneva Conference by John A. Hamilton, Deputy Assistant Director for Policy and Programs. He will be responsible for guiding the Agency's coverage of the Conference. Howard Garnish, U. S. Public Affairs Officer in Geneva, will be in charge of news coverage of the meeting and Jack Connolly, Deputy Director of the Motion Picture Service, will direct the Agency's filming activities. The Voice of America will have a special radio broadcast team at Geneva."

By some curious lapse the USIA press release described the Geneva meeting as the "Korean Political Conference."

Indo-China was forgotten in the Washington press handout. But, at Geneva, Korea was forgotten and a large part of Indo-China was lost to the free world!

Although a small army of USIA propagandists moved into Geneva under Streibert's command, the follow-up was nil. The recognized press spokesman for our nation at the Geneva meetings was the able and experienced Mr. Henry Suydam, Chief Press Officer of the U. S. Department of State, who skillfully maneuvered to make the best out of one of the most bitter diplomatic setbacks our country has ever experienced. The Geneva Conference was covered for the world-wide press by more than 1,000 legitimate reporters and radio commentators. This army of journalists did the work while the USIA "opinion molders" had the fun.

Mr. Jack Connolly, Deputy Director of the USIA Motion Picture Service, ordered the grinding of so much film footage at Geneva (films that will never be shown) that he accidentally had himself photographed with the arriving Communist Chinamen and had to edit himself out of his own films! Connolly enjoyed his own mistake!

The Geneva Conference experience highlighted another disquieting habit into which the USIA has fallen. This is the incorrigible habit of announcing *in advance* every strategic gambit which the United States is contemplating in its Cold War propaganda course. Every move is telegraphed to the enemy in italicized words. USIA press agents leak to the world press key facts which ought to be kept in inviolable secrecy from foreign eyes. While Soviet Russia, in Churchill's great phrase, remains a "mystery wrapped in an enigma," America's Cold War preparations are conducted in a USIA goldfish bowl.

What general, in command of vast armies, would reveal the facts about his fire-power, man-power, sources of supply, and plan of attack on the eve of an important battle?

In *Press Release No. 106,* dated August 2, 1954, Andrew W. Smith, Jr., former chief of the Motion Picture Service, came out with the striking announcement that USIA had just added 200,000,000 new overseas viewers to its cinema audience.

The statement, fed to the press associations, made headlines throughout the country. It was both newsworthy and impressive until it was revealed how Smith had arrived at this huge figure. Then the hoax was obvious. The USIA, it appeared, had sent prints of five of its propaganda shorts to the foreign offices of American theatrical film distributors. By this means, it hoped to obtain showings in movie theaters overseas. By "appropriating," in a *single* press release, the *entire* 200,000,-000 weekly overseas audience for Hollywood entertainment films, Smith was able to make this sensational claim!

What the USIA's Washington film director did not mention is the fact that no theater manager at home or abroad would, knowingly, inflict propaganda films on his patrons who have paid their money at the theater's box offices solely to be entertained.

Film Daily nailed the Smith whopper by pointing out that the 714 USIA prints, which were reported by Smith as in use, could not possibly add up to such an audience figure as 200,000,000.

Film Daily also pointed out a graver aspect of the announcement. If the USIA had made any such an arrangement with the foreign commercial exhibitors, it was doing a serious disservice to our whole Hollywood film industry. By identifying the USIA propaganda films with the non-political Hollywood entertainment output, suspicion would be thrown, in foreign minds, upon the whole Hollywood product, and its effectiveness as an expositor of the American way of life abroad would be seriously weakened. Since the Hollywood entertainment films are the greatest missionaries of Americanism abroad, this would be a particularly clumsy kind of public relations operation.

However, there is no record, to date, of any effort of the USIA to correct this egregious USIA misstatement.

In his speech before the International Advertising Association, the Director declared in outlining the policies and purposes of the Agency: "Both of us are in the business of making friends abroad. . . . The experience of earlier years has taught us not to talk too much

—not to try to tell everything about America—not to stress our material wealth to less fortunate people whose only reaction is misunderstanding, no understanding, or resentment."

Three months after the speech, the Agency launched its great Atomic Show in Rome, preceded by a fulsome press release. The Associated Press dispatch from Rome reporting the debut of the show said: "The world premier yesterday featured some fairly restrained pitchmen, a variety of gadgets that whirled and blinked lights and a few pretty girls."

A further dispatch from Rome to Washington radio commentator Ray Henle was reported on his news program, "Three Star Extra." It said: "The exhibit closed today. . . . Only a small percentage of the Roman population saw the exhibition and realized its peaceful scope. The general impression of the public, misled by the posters, was that at this particular moment it was extremely inopportune to recall to a frightened population something which, notwithstanding any possible peaceful use, is still and above all thought of as a deadly destructive force. The disfavorable impression was enhanced by two far-reaching searchlights circling nightly in the peaceful Roman sky, reviving memories of past air raids and raising fresh apprehensions for the future."

Press releases of the Agency stated that the show would visit 19 Italian cities, then visit 75 other lucky communities. A duplicate show was scheduled to open in France.

As the warmth of the summer fixed itself upon our Nation's Capital, the intensity of the USIA's press blasts increased. On July 2, a two-page press release (No. 94) marked for use on the day *after* the Fourth of July boldly announced:

"The U. S. Information Agency is intensifying its long-range world-wide effort to expose imperialist Communism as a harsh form of colonialism—Red Colonialism.

"In an instruction enroute today to the Agency's 217 posts in 76 countries, Director Theodore C. Streibert pointed out that Communist parties throughout the world are directly tied to Moscow and Peiping and that these ties can be demonstrated—"

The USIA's "demonstration" required a page and a half of single-spaced mimeographed copy!

Eighteen days after the Agency's release, Congressman Albert Rains (Dem., Ala.) noted the following account of NBC correspondent James Robinson who had just returned from Hanoi, Indo-China. This appears on Page A5226 of the Congressional Record of July 20, 1954:

"Let's take an example of how the Communists operate in the field and how the United States operates in the field in Asia. We'll pick an unnamed Asian nation yet free. We want this country as an ally, the Reds want it as a satellite. Here is how the operation goes.

"We pick a university graduate—clean-cut, intelligent, honest. His basic instruction is to go to this country and inform the people how nice democracy is—how bad Communism is. This man has never been to Asia, doesn't know the language. He arrives and moves into a lovely home, has servants, a car, and chauffeur and an air-conditioned office. And our man zealously goes to work putting out slick paper pamphlets about how nice America is and what rats the Communists are. Good stuff for readers in Kansas City, but remote to the man in the street in Asia.

"Now comes the Communist equivalent. First, he's an Asian, he speaks the local language, he lives with the people—in short, he is one of them, except he is highly trained —a specialist in Communist double-talk. When the Mr. Whong of Asia sits down in his local coffee shop, he meets this ardent Communist. But Mr. Whong doesn't realize this man is an agent. For this man speaks his language, talks of all the things bothering Mr. Whong and of course, adds his very cleverly planted seeds of revolt. A distorted picture? Unfortunately no. I wish it was.

"Force is still the deciding factor in Asia. This fact goes against our training and ideals. Not so with the Communists. They have force and are using it. At this late date we have but one choice—either we now move in and take over much of the control of Asia, or the Communists will. It's as brutally simple as that. If we're not willing, or able to do this, then the Communists surely will rule all Asia in the years to come."

Another USIA announcement that must have caused sleepless nights in Moscow is this globe-girdling gem: *Bulletin No. 8o,* two pages, single-spaced:

"A new world-wide offense, specifically designed to expose the spurious intellectual and ideological appeals of Soviet Communism, was launched today by the U. S. Information Agency. In a special instruction to all 217 overseas posts, Agency Director Theodore C. Streibert called upon field officers to devote maximum effort to the new program in order to bring out the fallacies and inconsistencies of the Communist orthodoxy. . . . As a first move the Agency has selected a shelf of 54 books representative of scholarly research and critical analysis of Communist doctrine, strategy and methods. . . . Books offer the best means of reaching these influential thinkers with cogent facts and documented arguments."

If the USIA were as effective on performance as on high sounding declarations of purpose, we might take the Director's words more weightily. Unfortunately, the implementing of the Washington projects quickly bogs down in the incompetent hands of the routineers who, with few exceptions, staff the Agency's posts overseas.

One of the most ignoble characteristics of these USIA handouts and releases, which flow so endlessly from Washington, is the breast-beating that they indulge in. The name United States Information Agency, spelled out in full, and usually the name of the Director or some other executive of the Agency, beckons to the eye conspicuously on every handout. Worse, the releases are undisguisedly proclaimed to the entire world as U. S. Government propaganda, thus losing their only slight hope of acceptance as bona fide news. Subtlety and public relations knowhow are certainly not notable USIA traits.

In *Press Release No. 100,* two pages, the USIA rushed in with a dispatch crediting itself and its Director with the news that there were food riots in China. Although there have been major food shortages in China for centuries, due to natural causes and overpopulation, the Agency saw fit to connect the disaster with the Communist state taking most of the farmers' crops. The Chinese farmer has been accustomed to shortages and the War Lords taking his grain for years and perhaps cannot distinguish as clearly as the USIA between the various oppressors. While the USIA was bemoaning the plight of the Chinese farmer, the American delegation at Geneva was trying to get itself out of the mess it had got into when it went there determined to meet with representatives of the government with which it had to make peace terms in the Far East. The New York *Times,* in an editorial, said: "Some of the troubles, floods and crop failures are not to be attributed to the sins of the Communist regime. For those who suffer, as so many Chinese have suffered, we have only compassion."

Aside from the questionable policy of gloating about disaster and the bad timing of the release, the question arises as to how this dispatch fits in with the pronouncement of "not haranguing the Communists" and of the President's objective of making known "our sound policies dedicated to the goals of peace, freedom and progress." Nor does it have anything at all to do with telling the world about America.

It may not be deception and dishonesty, in the accepted political code, for an agency to try to keep itself alive by a quarter-million-dollar ballyhoo to exploit itself to Americans, but stupidity can be more dangerous than dishonesty when it comes to exhibiting America before the eyes of the world.

The few examples given show the disastrous consequences of having two voices for a government—one the State Department, allegedly speaking the country's policies and ideals, the other the self-propelled, self-

praising loud-speaker engaged in propagandizing itself
to the American taxpayer while it continues to lose
friends for us abroad.

But the sobering thing to consider is what would
happen if, by any chance, the war that so many legislators say they fear, would come upon us suddenly; overnight we would find ourselves saddled with this sorry
group of non-professional newspapermen, tyro editors,
dream promoters and stunt providers who would become the official definers of American policy.

Big epaulets would give them an added authority that
they now lack, and bigger appropriations, under the
guise of patriotism, would lead them into further wild
extravagances of spending. But it would be the same
incompetent band who have bungled so hopelessly the
propaganda job of the peace.

10

Stassen's Slush Fund—The FOA

Not often do politicians admit that handouts to foreigners must come ahead of security for Americans.

But Harold E. Stassen made such an admission in a public statement on December 6, 1952, just after he had been selected by President-elect Eisenhower to head the Mutual Security Administration—soon rechristened the Foreign Operations Administration. Mr. Stassen has always enjoyed hearing himself talk and on this occasion he really pulled out all stops on American foreign policy.

His aim, said the Mutual Security Director-to-be, would be to bring about "peace and good living conditions for all the world's people." And, Stassen added, "We cannot, nor must we ever trim our aid to needy free nations just for the sake of *cutting our own budget.*"

From the start, the Foreign Operations Director has faithfully followed the dangerous doctrine of perpetual

American deficits, as long as a single "needy free nation" asks our dole.

In Washington, which so often resembles an Alice-in-Wonderland stagesetting, the prize exhibit is probably the presently named Foreign Operations Administration, *nee* Mutual Security Administration.

In FOA, waste and give-aways really reach the stratosphere. Where USIA picks the pockets of Americans in millions, FOA is up in the airy heights of the billions. For 1955, its budget was set at $2,781,499,816 in *new* cash and $2,462,075,979 in *carry-over* funds, totaling $5,243,575,795 for foreign aid for the fiscal year.

But this will only be a part of the actual cost of FOA to the nation. An accumulated *backlog* of grants, voted to FOA by previous Congresses, and which the FOA big brass have not had time to spend, approximates $10,-000,000,000—and $2,000,000,000 of this is unallocated!

The new money is appropriated before the old money is spent. All this folding money will be at the disposal of Harold E. Stassen and his billion-minded lieutenants.

FOA is a government spending agency which continues to exist, prodigally, long after its announced program has been completed. It symbolizes the self-perpetuating persistence of waste. President Eisenhower's urgent plea of June 24, 1954, that the 1955 FOA appropriation be passed by Congress without reduction doomed any hope of a realistic trimming of this fruitless program.

The American voters elected General Eisenhower to the Presidency in 1952 on his implicit pledge to wipe out waste wherever, under the lax hand of Truman, it had entrenched itself in our Government.

Particularly, they expected the quick liquidation of MSA, predecessor of FOA. Here, it was generally agreed, was one spot where billions could be lopped off without hurt to American well-being or without weakening of our national security.

Instead of getting the American people out of MSA, President Eisenhower promptly placed his stamp of approval upon it.

In the 83rd Congress he asked that it be prolonged for at least four years, in the face of Congress' demand that it be strictly limited to a one year operating period. The only notable changes which followed were a change in the name, from MSA to FOA, and a change in the directorship, from the ineffectual W. Averell Harriman to the egregious Harold E. Stassen. Opportunity to get the United States out of the foreign subsidy quagmire was tossed away.

To realize how far afield from its original purpose FOA has drifted, we have only to recall the grounds upon which its predecessors came before Congress for their huge appropriations.

First was the Marshall Plan, enunciated by Secretary of State George C. Marshall in June, 1947.

The Marshall Plan, as first proposed, had little or nothing to do with the omnibus activities which now cluster about the FOA holding company. The Marshall Plan proposed only that the United States should underwrite financially a cooperative plan for economic recovery that the nations of the world, including Russia, should themselves devise. The Europeans and Asiatics should make the plan and carry it out, largely with their own money. Our role was to supplement their efforts with American billions, with a minimum of supervision over its disbursement. The Economic Cooperation Act of 1948 was passed by Congress to carry out this Plan. Russia and its satellites, in the meantime, had refused cooperation.

As envisaged, it was to be a four-year plan, and then we were to get out of it. Unhappily, the termination date, 1952, is long past, but we are still in it, neck-deep.

What happened was the Korean war of 1950, which gave the ECA an excuse to demand another billion-studded program to follow ECA—the Mutual Security Administration. The emphasis in the new program was to be upon military, not economic, aid. And yet, so reluctantly do spending programs die, economic aid turned up again in the MSA program—$845,000,000 of it in the 1954 FOA budget.

When the Eisenhower Administration came into power, a further step away from the original objective was taken. FOA, in addition to the military assistance program, was set up as a loose administrative agency under which were gathered all the international aid program waifs and strays which had grown up under the umbrella of American Congressional appropriations. Today, in addition to Military Assistance, Mr. Stassen's FOA includes the following variegated functions:

Administration of (1) Technical Assistance (Point 4).
(2) International Development.
(3) UNRWA (Palestine Refugees).
(4) Special Economic Assistance to Palestine, Arab States and Iran.

(5) UNKRA (Korean Reconstruction Corporation).

(6) Relief for African Dependent Overseas Territories.

(7) ICEM (Movement of Migrants).

(8) Technical Cooperation Program of Organization of American States.

(9) Children's Emergency Fund, with United Nations.

(10) Escapee Program, Authorized by Kersten Act.

(11) Administration of the Battle Act.

To administer this cluttered program, a formidable army of "experts" and bureaucrats numbering in the thousands was recruited.

How do the partisans of the FOA program justify this huge bite which they are taking out of the nation's budget?

An arguable defense of FOA spendings would be that these billions have purchased security for the United States; that they have won for us dependable Allies who will stand beside us against the Soviet Russia-Red-China axis when we need them. It would be heartening to believe this, but the facts do not bear it out.

In a specific issue, such as Indo-China, we learn with chilling effect that none of the great powers which have enjoyed our successive aid programs is with us in the clutch. At the decision hour, we found ourselves alone with such feeble comrades as Thailand and Formosa.

Americans, with Podsapian optimism, reassure themselves that they have Allies. Actually, the Free World, with unimportant exceptions, is a neutralist world, and our World War II partners—Britain, France, Republican Italy—are cynically unwilling to make the hard and fast commitments to the United States that would close the door to possible future bargaining with a winning Communist other side.

When we take the longer view, the aid which we have poured out under ECA, MSA and FOA to such a politically unstable nation as France, for instance, may actually be a contribution to American weakness, rather than to strength.

France, with its outspoken anti-American extreme Left and extreme Right, and with its irresolute center, could easily pass into the hands of a government which is willing to make a deal with Russia, were the United States in serious danger. In that event, all our immense givings to France and to NATO could turn out to have been a contribution to the enemy. They would be scooped up by an advancing and occupying Soviet Army.

A picture of the quantity of these military stores which we have shipped to France and the other NATO countries was given by President Eisenhower when he reported that in the four years ending December 31, 1953, we gave these countries:

99,444 electronic and signal equipment items;
30,792 tanks and combat vehicles;
176,343 motor transport vehicles;
30,037 artillery pieces;
35,372,000 rounds of artillery ammunition;
601 naval vessels;
5,340 aircraft.

In sending these vast stores abroad, we have weakened American home preparedness, without any certainty that the material will not be used against us in our own hour of peril.

Similarly, the money and material which we have transferred in the last six years to such unpredictable nations as Yugoslavia, Italy, Egypt, Iran, India, Indonesia, etc. have been the sheerest gamble. We have given arms and economic development to nations which, while now friendly, are dangerously fluid in their politics. We haven't the slightest assurance, except in our own wishful thinking, that any or all of these fence-sitters will be with us when the showdown comes.

Another familiar contention of the foreign aid cult is that the United States actually has no other choice but to place these itching-palm nations upon our "give" list. Otherwise, it is asserted, they will be so weak economically and politically that they will slip over in internal disorder to the Communist side.

The argument has only to be examined to reveal its absurdity.

If the aided nations are so weak that they cannot exist, as viable non-Communist states, without being propped up by American dollars, what possible strength could they bring to the United States as Allies? In time of war, weak Allies, who have to be reinforced at the expense of the main theater of operations, are a liability, not an asset to a strong nation.

A classic instance was Italy in World War II. When, in the spring of 1941, Hitler was forced to divert forces from his assembling Eastern front mobilization to bail out Italy in its losing assault on Greece, he lost the all-important weeks which would have enabled him to complete his conquest of Russia before the arrival of winter. Without this diversion he might have crushed Russia. The decision of the whole war slipped out of his hands as a result of his alliance with weak Italy.

In the face of all military history, the strategists of the FOA are proposing to stop Communism by burdening the United States with a whole crew of devitalized and demoralized Allies.

This "save-our-Allies-from-collapse" argument, which has been the principal selling point of the foreign aid drum-beaters, is actually the clincher argument why we should quickly extricate ourselves from the whole rickety program.

America is strong, but certainly she is not strong enough to hold back world Communist aggression if she is to carry on her back every disorderly and bankrupt nation in the world. Today, to her sorrow, she has 46 retainer nations weighing her down.

Little wonder that Representative Brady Gentry of Texas asked pointedly in the House on March 22, 1954:

"How did our country get into such a horrible situation? Are we so helpless that we must be hijacked by everybody? Must we make a permanent mendicant of every nation in the world? Can it be possible that we, as a nation, are in the position of the plunger who, long after better judgment and prudence dictate more careful consideration of his course of action, continues throwing good money after bad?"

And four months later, Congressman Cliff Clevenger of Ohio, speaking from the floor of the House, said:

"I just want to tell you that budgets are not balanced by any other method than deciding what we can live without. What would you do in your own case and in your own household in passing on this stuff when you realize that every dollar that you now spend is deficit spending and must be laid on the shoulders of generations yet unborn? We have 7,000 little, new Americans every morning. You have $278 billion resting on these defenseless little children. I want to see the time come soon when a man will be glorified and not subsidized—when a baby can be born without being swathed in a wet blanket of debt, deficit and despair."

Although FOA and its predecessors have been ill-conceived and impractical in program, their most glaring faults have revealed themselves in administration. FOA-MSA-ECA, under the Hoffmans, the Harrimans and now the Stassens, have been conducted on such notoriously loose and unsound business principles that they would have quickly bankrupted any private, self-sustaining business.

One of the open waste drains in the program has been Technical Assistance, popularly known as Point 4. From its outset in 1950, Technical Assistance has frankly been a do-gooder, share-the-wealth program—a program of all give for the United States, and no get. Hailed with extravagant praise by all of the "One Worlders," it started as a bureau of the Department of State with an initial budget of $34,500,000.

From the beginning, Point 4 was President Truman's baby. It was his proud exhibit to which he could point when critics scoffed that the United States had no constructive alternative to Communism for undeveloped nations. It was a program which seemed to do something about world poverty. Commentators were loath to uncover its false pretensions lest they be open to attack as opponents of humanitarianism.

Under this immunity to criticism or analysis, Technical Assistance began to balloon. By 1953, when it was taken out of the Department of State and given to Stassen, its budget had swollen to $165,395,000. Even after a well-publicized economy drive, its budget still stood at $136,528,000 in the 1955 appropriation. Nor is this the whole story. The United Nations was simultaneously conducting a program in Technical Assistance. Since we are the principal UN underwriter, our 1955 bill for UN Technical Assistance comes to an additional $9,957,621. (President Eisenhower originally asked for $17,958,000.)

But Technical Assistance soon gave birth to a parallel program which was fated to become even larger than its parent. This was International Development, a title of pleasant connotation, under which Uncle Sam finds himself picking up the check for costly public works projects throughout the non-Communist world. When this program was launched, under the International Development Act of 1950, development assistance was only a free rider on the TCA appropriation. In the 1955 appropriation, development assistance was *separately* budgeted, and was down for a total of $224,000,000. When Rep. Alvin M. Bentley (Rep., Mich.) offered a motion that all of this amount be upon a loan basis, instead of half of it an outright gift, his motion was voted down.

If we take seriously the recommendations of the President's International Development Advisory Board, headed by Eric Johnston, the present spendings for development assistance are but the curtain raiser for the giant program that is to come. Under this program the United States is to be the underwriter for a great international WPA, with this difference—that after paying the bills, the United States won't own the projects. They will be the possessions of the aided nations.

For instance, in neutralist India, United States assistance to the tune of $85,000,000 for development, plus $19,500,000 for technical cooperation, is to be a part of India's Five Year Plan, with the title vested in India's government. While this is not as bad as the $236,000,-000 a year that Chester Bowles wanted to give Nehru, it is certainly not hay.

When he was asked why, in giving India several million dollars for railroad rehabilitation, he had not put it in the form of a loan, Director Stassen declared that India would find it difficult to repay the loan. Had he insisted on a loan, he said, it might have resulted in bad feeling between these two sister "democracies," so he just gave them the money. Spendings are that casual in the FOA.

A hint of the bottomless pit of United States spending which lies before us if we follow the Point 4 program to its logical conclusion was given by Dr. Ralph J. Bunche, who is himself an ardent advocate of underwriting overseas distress:

"In Asia, Africa, the Middle East, the Pacific and much of Latin America there are perhaps a billion-and-a-half men, women and children for whom, if in varying degree,

poverty, hunger, disease and ignorance are the typical way
of life, and few among them have ever known another."

It is frightening to think what will happen to the
hard-pressed American economy if Dr. Bunche's billion-
and-a-half underprivileged are to be added to the list
of American social responsibilities.

As we go through the confusing itemizations of
the $5,243,575,795 FOA fund for 1955, we are struck
again and again by the examples of financial laxity and
unreality that lie buried in the over-all totals.

Take, for instance, the item of $35,000,000 for Great
Britain to finance its manufacture of aircraft. President
Eisenhower originally asked for $75,000,000 for this
project, a reckless kind of military gamble. The United
States, after paying over the money, will have no follow-
up authority to enforce the use of this material for objectives which we desire. When investigators for the
Senate Appropriations Committee made an on-the-spot
investigation of how previous money given to the British for this purpose had been spent they found that
$75,000,000 of American money had been diverted by
the British from military uses to finance the development of commercial jet planes (the Comets) which compete with the American air transportation industry.

Or take the item of $250,000,000 which is authorized
for guarantee of American investors overseas against
losses from confiscation or currency nonconvertibility.
While it is generally agreed that bona fide American
investment abroad is a desirable end, investment which
is so hazardous that it must be insured by the government is not investment at all: it is merely a skillfully

packaged subsidy. American investors are to be encouraged to take risks, not on sound projects, but on ventures so dubious that they could not attract capital on their own merits. To encourage such uneconomic investment can aid neither the United States nor its Allies. It is a rathole operation. And yet Uncle Sam is laying $250,000,000 on the line for such Ponziism.

Another manifestly debatable item in the FOA 1954 and 1955 budgets is $115,000,000 for economic aid to Spain. While there may be sound strategic reasons for cutting in anti-communist Spain on the aid program, there is no excuse for FOA laxity in not exacting effective controls over the spending of the $115,000,000. We just hand it over and trust for the best.

One of the major indictments of the FOA and its subsidiaries is their slippery way of evading Congressional supervision. FOA chiefs have shown themselves adept at the art of the Congressional by-pass.

Although Congress has been frequently burnt by this bureaucratic habit, it neglected to take precautions against it in the Mutual Security Act of 1953. Instead it left an escape valve which practically nullifies Congressional checks on FOA outlay. By this act FOA administrators are permitted to transfer funds assigned for military assistance from one area to another up to 15 per cent. Such a provision is, of course, a blank check under which Mr. Stassen and his staff can juggle funds almost at will between areas and projects. No Congressional investigating committee could disentangle such bookkeeping.

On another front, Director Stassen has shown himself willing to disregard the express instructions of Congress, to meet the changing winds of White House foreign policy.

The issue has frequently arisen over the question of Russian and Iron Curtain trade. Under the Battle Act of 1951, Congress has clearly forbidden American aid to countries shipping strategic goods to Russia. Mr. Stassen is the administrator of the Battle Act. In April, 1954, Stassen, who was once granted an interview with Joe Stalin, began making noises indicating his approval of French and British plans to increase their trade with Russia.

When questioned by the House Foreign Affairs Committee on the Battle Act, Mr. Stassen went into a great outburst of double talk which left his hearers fully as much in the dark concerning his actual intentions as when he began. This passage is such a perfect example of FOA gobbledegook that it merits repetition as a Stassenism:

"So the effect of the new policy will be, as it is gradually worked out by technically-qualified people between the free nations, that those items that are highly strategic will be controlled more effectively than ever, in relationship to war potential, but a wider band of trade will be open to the Soviet area in Europe, in exchange for goods which they send out on a basis of making possible the expansion of peaceful trade, so that, in effect, we will be saying to the Soviet people and to the satellite peoples, 'If you move toward peaceful trade and away from a war build-up, there is an open door for trade,' and it may well be that in the long pull, the path to peace will be an economic road."

One would gather from the Stassen words that he conceives it as his task to redefine our national policy

regarding Iron Curtain trade, despite the fact that
Congress, in the Battle Act, has already prescribed it.
Mr. Stassen's thinking, according to his utterances, is to
pay lip service to the "strategic commodities" ban, just
as do Britain and France, but to thwart the will of Congress by redefining a long list of war-use goods as "non-
strategic."

Here again we have an arresting example of FOA
deliberate disregard of Congressional wishes in its disbursement of the swollen aid funds.

An impelling factor in the steady expansion of this
misbegotten Federal what-is-it is the concentrated determination of the FOA bureaucracy to remain firmly
glued to Uncle Sam's payroll. In the FOA job-holders
Washington has a determined and resourceful lobby
which has a vested interest in the year-by-year prolonga-
tion of the ruinous aid program.

Most of these men and women never had it so good
before.

Their salaries with the various FOA agencies are far
in excess of what most of them ever earned in private
stations, or can ever hope to earn again. In addition,
as they travel about the world, in first-class plane or
other accommodations, swelling their salaries with generous per diems, they have an inflated sense of power
as they hand out American benefactions to cringing and
obsequious foreigners.

Although FOA does not publish salary breakdowns
with the revealing detail of USIA, some typical instances will clarify the point. The Paris set-up is revealing. Here, on the verge of the consolidation of agencies
in the FOA, MSA maintained a staff of 395 Amer-

icans, served by a larger number of locals. Of these, 21
were on the payroll for $12,800 a year, not including
perquisites; 63 received $11,300 a year; 101 were down
for $9,130 to $9,950 a year.

On top of these salaries the foreign service employee
receives up to $3,000 a year for rental allowance for his
housing. There have been some economies here and
there during the last 18 months, but the basic situation
remains virtually the same.

As might be supposed, FOA and its predecessors have
been prolific publicity seekers. In the 1954 budget occurred an item of $7,600,000 for information. Wher-
ever MSA operated it maintained its own publicity
facilities, side by side with those of the USIA.

A third team of information officers was maintained
by TCA. Since MSA and TCA have been consolidated
into FOA, their information staffs are supposedly transferred to USIA. This is the theoretic situation. Actually,
FOA still maintains a staff of some noisy publicity
sharpshooters to publicize the ambitious activities of
Director Stassen. The handouts and booklets that issue
from the FOA offices are among the most voluminous
and verbose of any Washington department.

Another method which Director Stassen has employed to curry favor for FOA at heavy cost to the taxpayer is the sending of "teams" of business and civic
leaders to "inspect" FOA installations in the various
aided countries. In the face of public outcry against the
cost, Stassen has sent out 24 teams of evaluators to
various aided countries. Each team has traveled in luxurious style, accompanied by wives and secretaries. Mr.
Stassen, who is an unwearied political fence-builder,

has been able to reward influential Republican backers or prospective backers by inclusion on these junkets.

Any waste in FOA propaganda and publicity is now carried over to the USIA, and appears on its budget.

Both FOA and USIA are arms of the same operation.

Both are dedicated to the mission of selling the gullible American people on the virtues of a giant spending program to win dubious foreign friends for America.

The whole cumbersome USIA apparatus, with its mysterious high level support, keeps the American people softened up for the billion-wasting foreign aid program. A recognition of this key fact will explain many of the apparent stupidities in the current Washington information mess.

No one has put the case for the termination of foreign aid more cogently than did the President in his speech before the nation's editors on June 23, 1954. He said:

"The United States cannot be an Atlas, it cannot by its financial sacrifices carry all other nations of the world on its own shoulders, and we should stop give-away programs."

"Now, this is very true. You could not keep any other country in the world free merely by money. You can't buy or import a heart, or a soul, or a determination to remain free. Consequently, the statement that American so-called give-away programs are not going to keep the world free, is absolutely true."

Having made this sound pronouncement, the President virtually disavowed his position the very next day, on June 24, by sending a message to Congress insisting that the bloated $3,447,700,000 FOA appropriation be passed without reduction.

The Mutual Security program, he declared:

"Meets the Communist menace at the front line with practical and effective measures. . . . Having embarked upon these courses of action, we shall follow them through. We did not choose the gigantic struggle now endangering the world, but surely this is clear: during periods when the contest is hardest, we must not falter, we must intensify sensible and positive action."

Any reductions in the requested appropriation for the Mutual Security program, he said, "would be unjustified and unsafe."

A reconciliation of two such conflicting statements, made in the space of twenty-four hours, may be left to the judgment and personal reactions of the reader.

One of the most blasting commentaries on foreign aid, as now administered, was made by former President Herbert Hoover. The amount which we spend upon the FOA, reminded the former President, approximates the amount of the current national deficit. It is a measure of the complacency of present national thinking that American taxpayers would rather go billions of dollars into debt than trim the dead branches of FOA and USIA.

Or would they?

11

How They Put Over the Billion Programs in Washington

For sheer showmanship and political sleight of hand, the annual "put-over-foreign-aid" scramble is Washington's top performance.

Every year our Washington solons solemnly go through the motions of saying that this year is the last. But when next year's budget rolls around, foreign aid and information are back again, high on the White House "must" list. The high-pressure push to get the appropriation through the House and Senate with as little breakage as possible is resumed. Sometimes, disbelievers in the programs are able to set up troublesome roadblocks in the committees or on the floor. But in the end, the appropriations in full or generous part always go through—sometimes, however, at the cost of a changed name.

Mr. Plain American Citizen, who pays all the taxes,

must often wonder how the performance is negotiated. Since most of the fast footwork usually takes place behind scenes the question remains unanswered.

Take, for instance, the Congressional tussle over the 1955 information and aid programs.

By every rule of logic, 1955 should have seen both appropriations cut to the bone. The incoming Republican Administration was not responsible for either program. It had come into office in 1953 with a great mandate from the people to wipe out every vestige of Truman-Achesonism in foreign affairs, and to cut waste and extravagance. MSA and USIA were natural places to begin.

In its first year, the Eisenhower Administration had perfunctorily continued information and foreign aid for 1954, pending an opportunity to study both programs. But in facing the 1955 budget, the new administration was frankly on its own. It had the opportunity and the legislative time to do a realistic job.

What happened is now history. Congress gave the USIA $77,000,000 and FOA $5,243,575,795. In the case of FOA it did impose the proviso that the agency must end on June 30, 1955. But it is hard to take this proviso seriously when we recall that the 1954 FOA appropriation bill, passed by Congress in 1953, contained a similar proviso ending FOA on June 30, 1954. When the termination date approaches, there is always a convincing reason for prolonging the program for one more year.

Director Stassen, in charge of the biggest handout the world has ever known, is already preparing to perpetuate his Agency beyond the latest cut-off date ordered by Congress. This year, Mr. Stassen will argue that the need for money in Southeast Asia is greater than ever before. He will very likely proclaim solemnly that the vast pile of American equipment and supplies left behind to the Reds in Indo-China must be considered as left there for the benefit of the *people*. Stassen will not say to strengthen Communist people!

In the 1955 budget victory of FOA and USIA the decisive factor was the White House. At every important juncture in the extended legislative battle over these two programs, it was the White House which gave the "One Worlders" in Congress the extra oomph which put over the appropriations. It is a cold fact that the U. S. foreign policy is based upon giving money away.

The USIA had a particularly rocky path in both House and Senate in the second session of the 83rd Congress. This was decision year for USIA. The American public was beginning to tire of the unfulfilled promises of the information program. The Voice of America had been on the air, with spasmodic efforts, since 1942. The United States Information Service had been piddling around with its libraries and its International Press Service and its films since 1946, and earlier in its OWI version. Neither had emerged from amateurhood, and while they wasted time, world Communism was marching on.

With a current Federal deficit of $4,700,000,000 looming (according to the late-1954 estimate of the Secretary of the Treasury), a strong sentiment developed in both houses of Congress to lop off every unnecessary item from the $97 million first proposed for USIA in the President's budget of January 21, 1954. One place where it was generally agreed that a saving of $3 million could be made without cutting USIA effectiveness was in the motion picture operation. Enough documentary and other non-theatrical films were already on hand to serve foreign needs for at least ten years, without any new production. Another elimination which would save at least $6 million was the news cable which is now sent to 77 countries five days a week. Another $6 million could be saved by discontinuing costly USIA operations in countries such as Turkey, Spain, etc., where there is no existent Communist movement requiring counter-action.

Recognizing the opportunity for saving, the House Appropriations Committee, under the strong leadership of Chairman John Taber and Representative Cliff Clevenger, began chopping on the $97 million budget request. When they got through, the USIA appropriation was down to $75,800,000. Then the Senate took over.

With Republican control of the Senate at the time then resting on one vote, Senators were inclined to be more amenable to White House persuasions than the Representatives. The key Republicans on the Appropriations Committee on USIA matters were Chairman Styles Bridges and Senators Homer Ferguson*, Leverett Saltonstall and Karl E. Mundt. As co-author of the Smith-Mundt Act of 1948, Senator Mundt was generally regarded as one of the leading authorities on the U. S. information set-up and wielded especial influence in USIA decisions.

At the outset there was every indication that the

* Defeated for reelection.

Senate leaders were willing to go just as far as the House in cutting the USIA appropriation to the bone. Then the Administration got busy. President Eisenhower invited the key members of the Appropriations Committee to the White House, presumably to talk information program. The talk must have been very convincing. When the Senators got through with it they had given $8 million more to USIA than the House proposed. Instead of eliminating the totally wasteful film section, they had actually increased its appropriation over the 1954 total (1954: $3,390,000; 1955 Senate proposal: $3,-931,000). Other unnecessary activities were to receive even larger budgets.

A sad example of White House pressure was Senator Mundt. The South Dakota Senator was fully aware of the breakdown of the information program and seemed sincerely anxious to do something about it. Then the White House emissaries got busy on him. A candidate for reelection last year, Senator Mundt must have decided that the White House mind was so set on the information issue that only a costly intra-Republican struggle would result if he took a contrary stand.

In a letter to the author, written on January 21, 1954, Senator Mundt said:

"I also concur in the belief that the whole VOA* and USIA set-up should be revamped and restaffed and its activities rechanneled if this service is going to achieve the objectives for which it was established.

"I am confident, Mr. Castle, that when our Appropriations Committee next has before it the administrators of the

* Voice of America.

USIA a vigorous attempt will be made to reduce its expenditures and to try to channel its activities down the lines which were originally intended."

On May 29, 1954, he again wrote the author that:

"A lot of money is being wasted on phases of the Information Program.

"I agree completely with you that it was an error to take the USIS* out from under the Department of State and set it up as a separate agency. As you know, I opposed that switch at the time, but it was finally effected by an Executive Order issued by the President under the authority of the creation of the Hoover Commission. I thought then and think now that this move was a mistake."

To the author's amazement it later transpired that on May 7, 1954, three weeks earlier, Mundt had already filed a written statement with the Appropriations Committee declaring that:

"The critical times require that we should fully support the President's request of an appropriation of $89 million to carry out the overseas information program for the next fiscal year."

Under such pressures as may be imagined, the South Dakotan had completely reversed himself and capitulated to the White House. The incident is cited because the genial, pipe-smoking Mundt was regarded as being more independent than the ordinary run of Senators in Washington. What it does show is the appalling extent

* United States Information Service.

to which the information program has become the football of Capital Hill politics.

Another Senator who expressed concern with the present drift to the USIA set-up and particularly with the wasteful film program was the then Chairman Styles Bridges. He declared emphatically that he was against "bunching" appropriations for information. But when the 1955 appropriation came up, with all activities notoriously "bunched," Bridges, as chairman of the Appropriations Committee of the Senate, both sponsored and approved it. On June 15, 1954, a leading motion picture trade paper reported that Bridges had "revealed that the committee had defeated attempts to eliminate all funds for the film service and to cut the House figure in half."

This is the same Bridges who, on July 14, courageously introduced a constitutional amendment, jointly with Senator Byrd, forbidding the government to incur deficits, except in time of war.

Having scored such a striking success with the Senators, the Administration then went to work on the House leaders, in the hope that the House would accept the $8 million higher Senate figure for USIA when it reached conference. On July 3, the New York *World-Telegram and Sun* reported that President Eisenhower had made a direct personal appeal to Representatives Taber and Scrivner to restore the requested USIA funds which the House had eliminated.

The Presidential blandishments did not prove as effective with the Congressmen as they did with the Senators. When the representatives of the two houses met in conference, the House was adamant. Taber and

Clevenger accepted only $1,314,000 more for USIA than the $8,000,000 originally knocked out by the House. The final appropriation was $77,114,000—a disappointing come-down for the confident USIA-managers, but still nearly $40,000,000 *more* than is legitimately needed for American information to foreign countries.

The 1954 struggle was a fair sample of the maneuvering and jockeying for position which take place each year when the information budget is voted. The names change but the technique remains the same.

In the Congressional contest for another huge FOA appropriation for fiscal year 1955, President Eisenhower showed his hand more openly. From the onset, there was never any question that the FOA bill was a "must" White House measure.

The FOA was in a disadvantageous position in asking for new money, since it had almost $10 billion in unexpended funds on its books from past appropriations. Over $2 billion of this amount was not even obligated. Opponents could convincingly argue that FOA should first use up this huge backlog before requesting another appropriation. It was hard to persuade plain grassroots Americans that this was not possible.

The President came to Mr. Stassen's rescue. When it became apparent that legislators in both houses were ready to take the axe to FOA, the President on June 23 sent a special message to Congress forcefully asking that the full requested amount of $3,500,000,000 be appropriated, with no reductions or eliminations. The President's message followed an appearance of John Foster Dulles before the House Committee declaring that the passage of the bill was vitally necessary to our State Department plans. To reinforce Mr. Dulles, General Alfred M. Gruenther was brought over from Paris to impress upon Congress the desperate importance to NATO of continued heavy aid to our "Allies." In previous years at appropriation time, the personages of General Eisenhower and General Ridgway came from Paris headquarters to promote and plead for the renewal of give-away programs.

Before such pleas of urgency, Congress made only a slight reduction of the FOA appropriation. The Administration pressures saved the day for the aid program.

The whole history of the FOA and USIA agencies before Congress is full of such over-slick episodes. There was, for instance, the Hickenlooper Committee whitewash in 1953. The Hickenlooper Committee "to conduct an investigation and study of the objectives, operations and effectiveness of the overseas information programs" was authorized by a Senate resolution passed February 20, 1953. It followed a similar committee headed by Senator Fulbright in the preceding Congress.

Senator Hickenlooper is a Republican who can usually be depended upon to rubber-stamp White House wishes in any controversial situation. His committee, although appointed in the first economy weeks of the Eisenhower Administration, so far from recommending retrenchment, reported that the overseas information agencies "must and can be strengthened."

Hickenlooper's most notable idea, announced after televised hearings in New York, was that we needed an increase in our Voice of America programs in Latin America. Better informed men were at the same time coming to the conclusion that the VOA was doing us more harm than good in Latin America and the then Director, Robert W. Johnson, abolished the Latin-American broadcasts, pleading lack of funds. Subsequent events have confirmed the wisdom of Johnson's decision. However, Hickenlooper, loath to give up his idea, soon showed up in Argentina where he urged, in a news interview from Peron-land, an increase in American information activities—in a country virtually closed to American agencies.

The Hickenlooper report exerted an unfortunate influence upon Congress, for it effectively headed off an honest and unsparing "New Look" at the information establishment by the new Republican Administration.

As an example of the technique Senator Hickenlooper followed in preparing his recommendations, here are a few excerpts from a later hearing at which he questioned Mr. Streibert as head of the USIA. The Senator asked:

"What steps have been taken toward establishing a motion picture advisory group or otherwise securing the cooperation of the motion picture industry to lessen the number of objectional films sent abroad?"

Mr. Streibert replied:

"Since the extensive foreign distribution of United States motion pictures can make an important contribution to our information program, close liaison with the commercial motion picture industry is a continuing important aim of the Agency. In order to help the industry appraise its films in foreign distribution, the Agency makes available information concerning reactions to United States feature films, reported by our missions abroad. This information is forwarded to the Motion Picture Association for their use in considering requests to individual producers to limit the film's circulation. A continuing effort is being made to strengthen cooperation of the motion picture industry in regard to the subject matter and quality of films it distributes abroad. Cecil B. De Mille, a man who commands respect of the entire motion picture world, has accepted the post of Chief Consultant to the U. S. Information Agency. In addition, the following have voluntarily formed a committee to offer advice and assistance to the agency in connection with its motion picture activities: Frank Capra, Y. Frank Freeman, Edward Mannix, Milton Pickman, Gunther Lessing, Roy Brewer, Walter Pidgeon, Richard Breen, George Sidney, Carey Wilson, William Pine, Sam Briskin, Charles Brackett, Arthur Freed."

Mr. Pell Mitchell, an ex-newsreel editor living in Hollywood, attempted to contact personally the members of this committee and ascertain how active the advisory group was. Of the four members who were reached, three replied that they could not recall ever having been invited to a meeting or consulted, while the fourth had no comment.

It is transparently plain that this committee of impressive Hollywood names which Director Streibert refers to importantly when he is seeking new and larger appropriations is actually window dressing, with no actual function except to persuade Congress that his Agency is doing meritorious work. And yet Senator Hickenlooper, it appears, credulously accepted this souped-up statement from the head of the USIA!

Another authoritative-looking contributor to the current national confusion about the information program is the U. S. Advisory Commission on Information. This Commission, set up in 1948 under the Smith-Mundt Act, and appointed by the President, was originally created to provide an independent review of the program for the guidance of the President and as a frame of reference for information executives. For eight successive years it has never done so.

Its dominant figure was and is Erwin D. Canham of the *Christian Science Monitor,* one of the nation's great newspapers. Canham who, personally, has long been under strong "One World" influence, has been a starchy and respectable Boston front and apologist for the failures of the information program over the entire eight-year period. Ben Hibbs, able editor of the *Saturday Evening Post,* was, for years, a member of the Commission. Hibbs resigned in 1953 for reasons undisclosed and his place was taken by Sigurd S. Larmon, New York advertising agency tycoon and a leading "Ike Before Chicago" booster. Other members, more or less inactive, are Philip D. Reed of General Electric and Judge Justin Miller.

The Commission spent the relatively modest sum of $39,000 on its latest report, a small pocket-size leaflet that appears, all too obviously, to be the product of a professional staff, in which the busy members of the Commission probably had little hand. Even the headquarters of the Commission is in the same office as the USIA, which it is supposed to audit detachedly.

Under the reassuring names of the Commissioners, USIA has been able to pursue its career with a minimum of public criticism. The observation has been made that if the members of this rubberstamp Commission endorsed the same policies for their own successful businesses which they so complacently approve for the USIA they might all be in bankruptcy.

Wasting millions of dollars every year has become a fixed policy and procedure with our propagandists in Washington.

The USIA does not wait until June 30, the date when Congress makes its full appropriation available for the ensuing year.

Six months *before* the USIA is entitled to any new money, the Agency heads send urgent appeals to their employees, scattered all over the world, to prompt them to "dream up" the biggest, most expensive projects they can conceive and send these, post haste, to Washington to enable the Agency's directors there to rush to Congress with an emergency "appeal" for supplementary funds. These extra millions, supposedly to be spent for promotion "dreams" abroad, invariably never go beyond the paper they are written on!

But the great money-getting event is the annual budget.

Washington's big spending agencies carefully plan, many months in advance, how to influence legislators to increase their forthcoming budgets.

A "revitalized" campaign to influence economy-minded members of the 1955-56 Appropriations committees and, at the same time, to lessen complaints from American taxpayers, came into being with an announcement by Edward L. Bernays, freelance New York press agent, that he had formed a committee of 28 persons to propagandize the American people into thinking well of the United States Information Agency.

Never a shy one for personal promotion, Bernays appointed himself both chairman and chief spokesman for the group to be known as "The National Committee for An Adequate Overseas U. S. Information Program," with headquarters at the Bernays publicity office in New York.

In a press release issued on Monday, October 25, 1954, the objectives of the committee were defined as "stimulating international understanding of America, counteracting Communist propaganda, and strengthening bonds with our Allies."

Chairman Bernays further described his committee as an "educational, nonpressure group." When asked by Reporter Harold Hutchings of the Chicago *Tribune* whether the committee was formed to campaign for higher appropriations by the Congress, Bernays said that was not the plan. "We will not attempt in any sense to be a lobby," he said. But he added, "As far as I am personally concerned, $100,000,000 a year is an *inadequate* sum for this work."

Twenty-four hours *before* the release of the Bernays announcement, USIA Director Streibert in an interview commending both himself and his Propaganda Agency, which appeared in the Washington Sunday *Star,* highly approved the objectives of the Bernays group. An excerpt follows:

"Some members of the newly-formed National Committee for An Adequate United States Information Program, headed by public relations expert Edward L. Bernays, feel the Agency should have an annual budget of $125,000,000, *and the Director should have a Cabinet status."*

When questioned about this article, Bernays characterized it as "extremely unfortunate" and, he added, "makes it seem as if we're advocating a Dr. Goebbels for America."

In several of the press announcements relating to the committee, mention was made that Chairman Bernays was an associate of the late George Creel in World War I. Frequently, and over the years, Bernays has referred to this association.

George Creel was Woodrow Wilson's Director of Public Information throughout World War I. An independent Democrat, an adviser to Presidents, a famed author and journalist, Creel was truly a distinguished American of his era.

Just how well did Bernays know Creel?

In a profile of Bernays that appeared in the trade magazine *Advertising and Selling* for February 14, 1935, Bernays was said "never to have personally contacted the lovable Creel" while working for the Creel committee!

George Creel thoroughly abhorred and completely rejected the idea of the Government of the United States sponsoring "truth" campaigns to propagandize foreign peoples. He believed that such efforts would, in the end, only serve to make cold wars hot!

Also, Creel strongly opposed what he termed the "unsound, unsafe and un-American" idea of attempting to buy the loyalty of people overseas with unending giveaways. He minced no words in condemning these practices, as the following excerpts from an International

News Service dispatch of March 11, 1953, will plainly indicate:

WASHINGTON, March 11.—George Creel, U. S. propaganda chief of World War I fame, has bluntly rejected "insistent" suggestions from official sources that he accept a responsible role in a planned reorganization of the nation's present information program.

Creel's refusal is disclosed in a letter addressed to Sen. Taft and other influential Republican Senators who apparently had been urging that his experience qualified him for the job.

Creel, who headed President Wilson's committee on public information during World War I, criticized the Voice of America as "utterly ineffective" and blasted the whole propaganda effort since Pearl Harbor as a failure.

"In point of failure," he wrote, "our propaganda organization is without historical parallel, yet the President's directive gives the committee four months for study and report."

URGES REAL MESSAGE.

"The one hope," Creel continues, "is that Gen. Eisenhower will wake up to the fact that he has been tricked, and wipe out the whole bureaucratic extravaganza at once, and name one man to head one organization working with and under the President himself.

"And of course this one organization must have a gospel to preach instead of the hillbilly songs and meaningless prattle with which the voice has been cluttering world air lanes; a gospel that will carry hope to the enslaved, courage to the cowed and uncertain, and warning to the enemy that our faith still derives from the same dauntless Americanism that led plain men to risk all at Lexington and Concord.

"I have the deep conviction that Dwight Eisenhower can and will give us that gospel."

'RECORD OF FAILURES.'

Reviewing what he calls the record of failures, Creel says:

"A clutter of agencies, spearheaded by the OWI, spent millions between Pearl Harbor and V-J Day, yet victory found our world position so precarious that it was decided to continue the courtship of other nations on an even more lavish scale.

"When the Voice of America proved utterly ineffective, Radio Free Europe and Free Asia were hastily added, both supposedly supported by public subscription but secretly aided by federal funds.

"With success still elusive, a rash of "psychological" boards were midwifed, and more millions poured into the fight.

'CAN'T BUY FRIENDS.'

"And with what result? Since the war's end Moscow has added China, Bulgaria, Romania, Hungary and Czechoslovakia to her list of enslaved states; started the fires that now rage in Korea, Malaya, Burma, Indochina; turned Iran, Egypt and North Africa into powder kegs; changed Latin-Americans, our traditional allies, into greedy neutrals, and blocks the integration of Europe by occupation of East Germany.

"Where are our victories? So far from winning friendship, England, France and India prove that we haven't even been able to buy it. . . ."

A month later, in April 1953, at San Francisco's Bohemian Club where Mr. Creel lived up to the time of his death in October 1953, he told this writer:

"President Eisenhower was 'betrayed' when a group of 'stiff' shirts and self-publicity seekers who have never done a creative (editorial) job on a daily newspaper during their entire lives, recommended to the President that he establish TWO totally unnecessary NEW Government Agencies.

"You mark my words, Gene, these two bad will-milk-the-taxpayer-sucker setups will, in the end, help to turn the Government back to the Democrats. And I am a Democrat who turned Republican in the 1952 election—to take the Government out of the hands of the radicals who disgraced both my country and my Party."

But this new touch to get more money for the USIA via the Bernays committee can hardly be classed with the new twist that Director Harold Stassen has conceived to enable him to perpetuate his Foreign Operations Administration.

In the fall of 1954 Stassen's press department announced that arrangements had been completed to enlarge the direct participation of our nation's colleges in the Point 4 program.

To this end, the FOA Director set aside an initial sum of $15,000,000 for payment to colleges which would henceforth furnish both ideas and manpower for Point 4 extension overseas. At first glance, this appears to be a nice, cozy little arrangement. But, after more careful scrutiny, the real meaning of Stassen's idea comes to the surface! Actually, Stassen was subtly practicing the un-American method of subsidizing our institutions of higher learning.

On November 1, 1954, Stassen announced that 50 colleges had been enrolled in the program.

Although Stassen probably will deny it, he is paying for a college lobby and professor pressure group to adopt resolutions and transmit timely appeals to the Appropriations committees of Congress when the new Foreign Operations Administration budget is offered for debate and final decision.

When the $15,000,000 is spent will the colleges get more if Stassen doesn't? Do the colleges understand this? Could they use another $15,000,000? If so, may they not be expected to rally around when Stassen or his successor asks for more?

The plain reasons for the continuation, year after year, of topheavy appropriations for such completely unjustifiable government ventures, despite the financial burden they impose and even in the face of campaign promises to the contrary, may be summarized as follows:

The few Congressmen who make a brave initial, or at least vocal, show against wasting huge sums are quickly brought into line by what is politely termed "White House appeal," or, in other words, pressure from the President or his White House advisers, or both. The pressure may be directed through floor leaders, or by the more flattering White House luncheon. The balky legislator is reminded of patronage for his State or District, withheld or denied if he shows too much obstinacy. He is also sternly reminded of what party he belongs to and how necessary is conformity. "In these critical times," is usually added as a clincher.

Secondly, there is the trading on the head of the pork barrel, a custom that has increased, from a modest start, with the growth of the country. Again the recalcitrant Congressman, who honestly believes that the appropriation is way out of line, or padded, or even unnecessary, is reminded of one of his pet projects. There is that little item on House Bill No. XYZ23: to spend $10 million on Little Skunk Creek Dam—an engineering project that will be of small benefit to anyone except the reluctant Congressman running for reelection. So, on the next roll call, the well-intentioned legislator switches his vote. The popular name for this is logrolling.

The third reason, and most dishonest of all, is the common practice by agency heads of last-minute spending of unused and unobligated funds left over from the previous year's appropriations. When these unused funds are concealed and the whole amount asked for is granted under pleas of need, or dire necessities, the particular department of the Government is in deep clover. But sometimes, as occurred in July, 1954, the unspent funds are brought to light and the honest economists among the legislators call for a showdown.

An INS dispatch of July 27 states that the House Appropriations Committee sent to the House for debate an item of $2,896,000,000 in *new* funds, and authorization for the spending of $2,312,000,000 in unobligated money previously granted. The Committee charged that in a last-minute effort to show that the FOA really needed all it asked for, buying had been stepped up to get rid of the "hot" money. As an example, $72,000 was spent June 30 on office equipment, including 600 waste paper baskets. Another instance of wanton extravagance was revealed under the caption of "The Stassen Follies" when the Chicago *Tribune* made this terse editorial comment:

"Harold Stassen's latest operation to shovel the money out of the window calls for spending $833,000 of your tax money over the next three years bringing foreign cops to America for a post-graduate course in sleuthing.

"Our own law enforcement agencies have their hands full keeping up with domestic crime, and it seems superfluous to start worrying about stickups in Marseilles, Beirut and Rio."

Examples could be added by the hundreds—enough anchors to outfit the navy for 100 years, enough tire-chains for jeeps for a century of perpetual snow.

In no American enterprise, except Government, would such flagrant dishonesty be condoned. A bank or railroad official could not follow such practice without going to jail.

Only the passage of a Federal law can outlaw this indefensible practice of permitting unexpended surpluses to accumulate in the hands of squander-minded Washington agency heads.

The Washington story of the information and aid programs is a depressing story of inefficiency, waste, and irresponsible White House and Capitol Hill approval. Those who have beaten their brains out trying to do something about it have found themselves stopped at every point in the game, by a stacked political deck. Nothing less than an informed and determined demand for change by the long-suffering taxpayers of America will ever shake the political backers of these unconscionable programs from their present complacency and smugness.

12

Germany—Where America Has Tried Everything

It is in occupied Germany that our information story parts company with plain common sense and enters the realm of the farcical.

In Germany all the stupidities that we have encountered elsewhere in the information and foreign aid programs have been compounded and distorted. Germany is reparations land, where the millions are tossed about carelessly, not because we really expect them to accomplish anything, but merely because we have to get rid of the counterpart funds.

To get a true focus on the information story in Germany, it is necessary to review briefly the whole occupation comedy of errors since 1945. Human history supplies few parallels for the hasty and disorderly about-face which we have executed in virtually every initial policy with which we entered Germany.

To cite a few of our more sensational flops:

(1) We started out with a joint American-Russian-British-French occupation. Within two years we were on the point of war with our Russian "ally" and had replaced Germany with Russia as our No. 1 enemy.

(2) We began by collaboration with the German Communists. For the first two years we openly used them as our de-Nazification agents. With an abrupt change, we launched a purge which swept the Reds out of all posts of authority in West Germany.

(3) First, we attempted to reduce Germany to a second-class power by dismantling her industry and restricting her production. We followed this by a frantic and costly effort to rebuild and expand the German economy—an effort in which the United States has poured $3,250,000,000 into Western Germany in economic benefits.

(4) An initial step of the occupation was to demilitarize Germany. We are now remilitarizing her in such precipitate haste that some have even considered seriously the replacement of France by Germany as our No. 1 Continental military ally.

If we had started out to do so, we could not have come full circle more completely.

The picture of Uncle Sam's record in Germany during the last nine years is a fantastic muddle of swagger, of vacillation, of retreat, and always—of lavish and ostentatious waste. Barring a few heart-stirring highlights, such as the Berlin airlift, it has little to awaken American pride.

So many Americans have come and gone in Germany since 1945, each with a shining new German solution in his briefcase, that most of their names are now little more than footnotes. A few—General Clay, General

Draper, General Howley—have left Europe with heightened luster. But for most Americans who have labored in the occupation, Germany has been a reputation graveyard. No spot in the foreign service has been more withering to stuffed shirts.

All who have gone into Germany have quickly found themselves smack up against an impossible situation. That situation results from the fact that Washington actually has no German policy. Our administrators, from Clay to Conant, have found themselves whipsawed by constant shifts and reversals in their Washington directives. At best they have tried to make the oscillating directives work. At worst, they have simply coasted in futile self-importance. Meanwhile, the German problem has continued unresolved.

Nowhere has this drifting German policy exhibited itself more glaringly than in the information activities.

As we look back upon our nine occupation years, three distinct periods detach themselves.

The first, which lasted between two and three years, was the period of the pro-Russian honeymoon. As we recall the "Trust Stalin" years, they seem now like a bad dream—like a page stripped from Lewis Carroll.

During those first years, when theoretically there was a Four-Power Control Council at Berlin, some highplaced Americans in Germany did everything possible to turn the Reich over to Communism. Instead of attempting to restore normality, they conceived it their duty to conduct a moral purge, a Marxian revolution in the conquered country. By de-Nazification, they not only banished from political life the actual Nazis, but they extended their purges to millions of other Germans who had been involuntary Nazis with no actual sympathy for Hitler and who would have constituted a natural conservative German bulwark against the Communists.

By de-cartelization they attempted to break up German industry and banish it from the world markets. By reparations they sought to strip heavy German industry of its machinery and to trans-ship the machinery abroad to Russia, the satellites, and other allied countries.

The objectives of these Russia-firsters were aided by the wide American acceptance at the time of the vengeful Morgenthau Plan (even General Eisenhower was then calling for a twenty-year German penance period). The stronghold of the Morgenthau Planners was in the information agencies. American information officers were under stern instructions until 1947 to permit no criticism of Soviet Russia to appear, either in our own publicity or in the American-licensed German press and radio. Of course this meant that nothing effectively American-slanted could be said by our information agencies. The most sensitive years, when the numbed German mind was open to us for conditioning, America-wise, were thrown away by this stupid policy.

The information job in Germany, immediately after the war, was exclusively in the hands of the American Military Government. An Information Control Division was set up to administer it, under General Robert A. McClure. Hastily thrown together after the German collapse, ICD became a magnet for pro-Communists, alumni of the OWI, together with Left-minded intellectuals of all categories.

For a time, the most influential individual in information activities was Telford Taylor, whose actual job was chief counsel for the AMG war crimes office. Taylor, who likes to cover a lot of territory, suffers from a curious ambivalence which often prevents him from making a true appraisal of Communist activities. A New Dealer since 1934, he saw nothing un-American in sending a letter to the late Harold L. Ickes asking him to associate himself with the defense of the 11 top-flight Communists who were tried and convicted before Judge Medina in 1951. A New York newspaper published the text of Ickes' declination on February 9, 1952, citing Taylor's letter.

Taylor, as one of the Nuremberg prosecutors, pulled a lot of weight in Germany in 1946 and 1947. He was a strong advocate of using the German Communists to help the United States in de-Nazification. One of the Communists whom he reportedly used was an Austrian DP named Martin who secured the office of Political Intelligence Officer for Bavaria for the AMG. Martin was denied admittance to the United States in view of his Communist record. He was sent on a tour through Germany, wearing an American uniform and exhibiting a documentary film, "People's Court," to persuade the German people of the fairness of the Nuremberg trial.

Through its licensing authority, ICD exercised life and death power over German newspapers, magazines and radio stations. Also, ICD had the disposal of funds to subsidize favored German publications.

By some strange maneuvering James Aronson, an ex-OWI staffer, became the Civilian Press Control Officer of ICD. Aronson later was to become executive editor of the *National Guardian,* Communist party-line publication in the United States, and in 1953 he pleaded the Fifth Amendment before the Senate Investigations Sub-Committee. In Germany his recommendations resulted in the granting of licenses to open Communists to operate four daily newspapers, in Berlin, Heidelberg, Kassel and Wiesbaden.

Associated with Aronson, also as Press Control Officer, was Cedric Belfrage, a British subject. Belfrage was to become editor, with Aronson, of the *National Guardian,* and he also pleaded the Fifth Amendment when questioned by the Senate Committee. Through Belfrage's activities, German Communists were given license to operate the *Frankfurter Rundschau,* one of the most influential dailies in the American Zone, with a circulation of 150,000.

Another ICD officer was Arthur D. Kahn, chief editor of intelligence. Kahn, an open advocate of Soviet friendship, was later to write a Communist-slanted book on Germany which was published in Communist Poland and shipped to the United States for distribution through the Communist Party.

General McClure unintentionally aided the ICD Leftist clique in their efforts to win control of the newly formed and subsidized German-American news agency, DENA, by appointing Red sympathizers to its board; they chose, as a top licensee of DENA, Dr. Rudolf Agricola, a top Communist since 1933.

Likewise, Communists were installed in the key radio stations in the American Zone. The Frankfurt radio station was put under the control of Dr. Hans Meyer, head of the Communist "Protective League of German Writers." The Munich station was placed under the direction of the Communist Bentschen.

Although the Communists had few genuine followers in the American Zone at this period, many of the political officers of the AMG followed the incredible policy of trying to force them as leaders upon the German people. The officers justified this amazing course by arguing that Communists, because of their bitter hatred of Hitlerism, could be trusted to walk parallel with Americans in the de-Nazification of Germany. The inability of the German Communists to stand on their own feet in Western Germany was shown by the quick collapse of all their authority as soon as the American occupation heads withdrew support from them in 1947.

At the same time, in other AMG agencies, men of pronounced Leftist slants were securing footholds during this period. Max Lowenthal, Truman intimate and man of mystery, who was later to write a book smearing the FBI, was sent to Germany by some strange Washington influence as an adviser to General Clay, carrying a letter from Dean Acheson instructing all State Department officials to give him assistance. George Shaw Wheeler, who later renounced his American citizenship and went behind the Iron Curtain, was an official of the de-cartelization office. Director of investigation for the de-cartelization office was Russell Nixon. Nixon had previously been counsel for the Communist influenced United Electrical Workers, and after he left Germany, he returned to his union post. In the Treasury Department at Washington at the same time was Irving Kaplan, in charge of de-cartelization policies. Kaplan's repeated recourse to the Fifth Amendment, when questioned about his Communist connections by a Congressional committee, later led to his discharge from the UN secretariat.

Also in the Treasury Department was Harry D. White who, in a document on German policy drafted in 1945, which is now in the hands of a Senate investigating committee, recommended that 500,000 Germans be sent to Russia and other devastated countries as forced labor and part of German reparations. Fortunately, President Truman, at Secretary Stimson's urging, rejected this white slave labor plan.

On the Nuremberg trial staff was Mary M. Kaufman, assistant prosecutor, who was later the counsel for the second-string Communist defendants at the Foley Square trials, and who has appeared in numerous other strictly Communist Party court cases. Also on the Nuremberg prosecuting staff were Otto Verben and Kurt Ponger who were to be arrested in 1953 in Vienna for spying on behalf of the Communists.

These and numerous others set a poisonous climate of pro-Russianism in some of the branches of the AMG establishment. Although other Americans in Germany were watchful to oppose these Communist infiltrators, in the absence of a firm Washington policy it was difficult to stop their wide-ranging activities.

This first and Communist-oriented period came to an abrupt end with the Berlin airlift conflict. Washington awoke with a sick heart to realize that Russia was becoming an enemy of the United States and not its ally. Most of the Morgenthau Planners and the pro-Communists made quick and involuntary departures from the AMG payrolls. The industry dismantling, the de-cartelization and the more punitive aspects of the de-Nazification program were quietly dropped. A new attitude toward Germany gradually developed, foreshadowed by Secretary of State Byrnes' Stuttgart speech in September, 1946. Slowly the idea gained acceptance among Americans and British that Allied security demanded that Germany be preserved as a strong, highly productive Western-oriented area. When the ECA was launched in 1948, the new concept had replaced the Morgenthau mentality among Americans in Germany.

The second period, which saw ECA, NATO, EDC and the European Coal and Steel Community taking shape, was a period of Free World mobilization against Communism, with Western Germany included as an ally, not an enemy. This period saw a vast development of U. S. information and propaganda agencies in Germany.

Overnight, information and propaganda became a major activity of the highly touted "Cold War" against Russia in Germany. The idea gained general acceptance that we could use the channels of mass communication—the press, the magazines, the movies, the radio —in a massive assault on Communism, in the battle for the German mind. The task passed from the fumbling hands of the AMG into new civilian agencies which, assumedly, would bring an expert touch to our propaganda efforts. An ambitious and top-heavy staff of editors, writers, researchers, psychological warfare specialists, radio men, etc., was assembled in Berlin, Frankfurt, Munich and in other key German points.

Many of them turned out to be square pegs in round

holes. They were full of plans and projects for spending money, but they had little knowledge of the German people, and their earnest, hastily planned efforts often fizzled.

True, this second crop of informationists was an improvement on the sorry ICD pro-Communists, but only too many of them replaced the "trust Stalinism" of their predecessors with stuffy, self-righteous Achesonism which was equally offensive to all the German people who were not on the American payroll. (At one time, German locals on the American payroll in Germany totaled 450,000!)

However, the one project which generally was hailed as the most effective informational counter-weapon against Communism in Germany was an Army show. This was on Berlin radio station RIAS. While the State Department's "Voice of America" was making its ineffectual efforts over short wave, with the aid of relays, RIAS with its strategic Berlin location, 100 miles within the Russian zone, was speaking across the Iron Curtain to a potential listening audience of 40,000,000 over a wave length that their receivers could pick up.

Although RIAS was set up in 1945, its initial direction was so incompetent that it exercised little or no influence during its first two years. Its policy was to give "objective" reporting, which meant avoiding any direct anti-Communist broadcasts—in line with the ICD play-along-with-the-Communists policy of that period.

The man who revitalized RIAS and made it a battling force in the Cold War was General Frank L. Howley, Military Government Commandant in Berlin. Howley placed the station in the hands of capable men who

knew the score against the Communists, and who had
the courage to fight. William F. Heimlich, Boris Shub,
Gunther Neumann, Erik Ode, and Varady were some of
the talented group which made RIAS a continuous hair-
shirt to the Russians during the Berlin airlift months.

What made RIAS stand out in welcome relief against
the dreary background of spiritless information projects
into which American money was flowing was the quality
of imagination which animated it. Howley and his assistants recognized that RIAS was the most effective
wedge in their hands against Russian rule in East Germany.

One of their smartest stunts was to broadcast at
intervals to the East Germans the names of the Germans who were working for the Russian MVD, from lists
which were regularly supplied them by the anti-
Communist underground. Another was the frustration
of Russian plans for a "Ja" vote in East Germany in the
disappointing election after the blockade. The whole
career of RIAS during the uncertain blockade months
was filled with such incidents.

RIAS operated later in Berlin, under the supervision
of HICOG, but it has never quite repeated the high exploits of the airlift period. The top point of militancy
was indisputably reached during those tense months.
With the end of the crisis, the team broke up and less imaginative men took hold. At this writing, RIAS broadcasts a 22-hour program which, in addition to the regular
Voice of America programs, carries its own American-
slanted news and discussion features. It has attached to
itself a devoted body of German hearers who look upon
the station not so much as an American but as a Free

Berlin voice. The essentially local flavor of RIAS has been preserved by a predominant use of Germans on the staff—of approximately 600 employees, only 7 are Americans. For this, HICOG spent approximately $3,000,000 a year. Fair-minded observers will agree that it was probably the most productive $3,000,000 expended in the whole information program.

The third, or post-Berlin airlift, period—through which we are passing now—has seen America's information program in Germany settled down to a pedestrian, semiprofessional and highly expensive operation. The crusading fervor of the airlift period, while it exists in name, has slowed down to a routine gait. America's German agencies are crowded with high-salaried, careful-minded men, with a higher than average quota of incompetents and phonies who clamor constantly for increased Federal spendings to support the sprawling and, for the most part, wholly superfluous activities which they have spawned.

For 1954, the U. S. budget carried an appropriation of $39,966,700 for support of the civilian activities in Germany under the HICOG office. Of this, $20,974,340 was budgeted for the Public Affairs program which includes the information agencies. While this is a reduction from the high cost levels of the Truman years, it is still staggeringly and inexcusably high in terms of results. To administer the HICOG offices, a staff of 1,000 Americans and 4,698 local employees is maintained. This executive staff could very easily be cut 75 per cent, and such a reduction might very well bring about a much greater degree of efficiency.

The most obvious change in the German set-up was

the transfer in 1954 of direction of the Public Affairs program from HICOG to the new independent USIA agency. This has resulted in the budgeting of the Public Affairs program for 1955 in the USIA budget. However, since five-eighths of its cost is defrayed, not from direct Treasury appropriations, but from the occupation costs borne by the German government, the USIA figure for Germany reveals only a part of its actual size. That this change will result in increased economy or efficiency is extremely doubtful, in view of the boondoggling spirit of USIA.

The chronic fault of our Public Affairs bureaucrats in Germany has been an insatiable itch to launch an ever increasing number of continuing projects. Such projects make up an imposing grand total of work at the end of the year in the annual reports to Congress, but it is impossible to justify most of them on any scale of even partial proven results. They reflect the quantitative rather than the selective and effective approach to the information task, which is so alluring to the amateur.

Our $20,974,340 for "Public Affairs" in Germany includes such continuing tax traps as:

(1) Maintenance of 22 cultural centers, or "Amerika Haüser" in Germany; a highly questionable item;
(2) Publication of a daily newspaper, the Frankfurt *Die Neue Zeitung*, whose Berlin edition, with 666 employees, is now in process of transformation into a weekly;
(3) Publication of a monthly magazine, *Der Monat*;
(4) Publication of a weekly theoretical magazine, *Ost Probleme*. There is no reason why the American peo-

ple should subsidize the foreign press in West Germany or anywhere else;

(5) Maintenance of a film branch at Munich, with a budget of $2,082,783—$1,050,000 of which is allocated to the production of new documentaries; a ridiculous and wholly unsupportable waste of money;

(6) Maintenance of a "Special Projects Fund," with DM* 54,808,000, to give money to educational and social welfare agencies in Germany;

(7) Maintenance of the "Garica Press Fund," with DM 15,000,000, which has made loans to 85 approved German newspapers;

(8) Issuance of the "America Service," a daily wire, feature and photo service for German newspapers, and of a secondary service, DIMITAG;

(9) Maintenance of a "Radio Monitoring Unit";

(10) Issuance of a twice weekly mail "Feature Service";

(11) Maintenance of a "Photo Library";

(12) Maintenance of a "Press Analysis Section";

(13) Maintenance of a "Reactions Analysis" staff to make public opinion surveys;

(14) Maintenance of a "Pamphlets Section";

(15) Maintenance of a "Radio Branch," to coordinate RIAS and VOA;

(16) Maintenance of a "Public Liaison" office to assist press correspondents;

(17) Maintenance of 40 "Information Center Libraries";

(18) Maintenance of a "Book Translation Service";

(19) Maintenance of an "Exhibits Section";

(20) Maintenance of a "Speakers and Artists Bureau";

(21) Maintenance of an "Exchange of Persons Branch";

(22) A "Cultural Attaché" and staff, to promote the re-

* Deutschmark.

education of the German people along democratic
lines;

(23) Disbursement of "Grants-in-Aid";

(24) Maintenance of "Education Service" centers to induce "school reform" in Germany.

Most of this long list of propaganda projects are
plainly omnibus undertakings, which have been thrown
into the Germany Public Affairs program to magnify
activity and to justify cushy jobs for staff members. Any
honest overhauling of the Germany program would
prune away the largest part of these projects as superfluous and money-wasting. The Eisenhower Administration had a unique opportunity to do such cutting
when it assumed power. But while a very few economies
were affected, the dead weight of bureaucracy dis-
couraged any thorough-going attack upon waste. The
German propaganda circus continues, with good and
bad alike receiving a new lease on life.

One foe of economy or even strict bookkeeping in
Germany has always been the *Deutschmark* windfall—
the counterpart contribution in local currency made by
the Bonn government, ostensibly for the economic rehabilitation of Germany. As we have seen, this makes up
the greater part of the funds which are at the disposal of
our information program in Germany. Since *theoretically* it represents no cost to the United States Treasury, there has been a continuous temptation to spend it.
And, regardless of its ineffectiveness, the spending goes
on.

The devious ways by which these counterpart funds
have been expended would require a longer book than
this to record. One easy outlet has been building. Ameri-

cans in Germany are housed, at DM expense, in luxury that few ever enjoyed at home.

One housing extravaganza that is extremely hard to justify is the vast Plittersdorf project, outside Bonn, with 458 apartments, schools, a church, a theater, a shopping center and recreation building, which was erected at a cost of $28,000,000—an American luxury exhibit which is a flaunting mockery to the ill-housed German people. Each of the 458 apartments cost $21,000 to build, plus $5,000 each for furnishings. The equivalent could be built in Washington for $9,400 per unit.

In this same Bad Godesberg American enclave, residences for the High Commissioner, the HICOG Executive Director, the Deputy High Commissioner, the Director of the Office of Political Affairs, the Assistant High Commissioner, and the Chief of the MSA Mission were erected. The scale upon which housing was provided for these American high-ups is indicated by the $227,000 cost of the High Commissioner's residence, and the $115,000 cost of the houses of the other five officials. All were supplied with furniture imported from England at a cost equivalent to $126,000.

When it is recalled that Bonn is only the temporary capital of Germany, and that the whole Bad Godesberg location may be valueless to American diplomats within a few years, the recklessness of a building program on this scale is apparent. The Bonn development was on top of the construction of a 420-unit apartment house for American functionaries at Frankfurt, completed in 1950. The HICOG proceeded determinedly with these housing projects despite the fact that the General Accounting Office seriously questioned its authority to spend counterpart funds for such a purpose in the absence of a specific authorization by Congress.

The whole incident is a graphic illustration of the way in which the occupation authorities have irresponsibly squandered the counterpart funds, rather than return them, when unneeded, to the Germans. When doubt arose whether the $1,090,000,000 allocated by the Bonn government to American occupation expenses in 1953 could all be spent before new agreements with Germany placed the occupation army on a pay-as-you-go basis, it was reported that Army authorities engaged in an unrestrained purchasing spree for unneeded household equipment, painting and renovation of apartments and other waste. Anything to get rid of the money.

Still another American agency bulks importantly in the German picture. This is FOA*. FOA does not maintain a program for West Germany, where economic aid is now not needed, but it does have an economic relief program for Berlin. Although no shipments of military goods are now made to Western Germany, MSA representatives have set up a tentative program when and if a reasonable substitute for the ill-fated EDC is ratified, and stockpiling for Germany has been initiated under this program. Little specific information concerning FOA Germany plans has been made public.

Although there are some redeeming lights in the German picture, the over-all impression is one of inexcusable floundering in the face of an historic opportunity. It took the United States almost three years to discover the actual nature of the American task in Ger-

* Foreign Operations Administration.

many, and to shake off the vapors of the "Russia-our-ally" delusion. Once we awoke, we moved energetically in the Berlin crisis, but our information program has bogged itself down in a multiplicity of prissy projects and attempted thought controls, and has become a method of spending money just for the sake of spending it.

Where it has encouraged the German people to act for themselves, it has been at its best. Where it has relied upon the ex-parte judgments of the inadequate experts whom we have shipped to Germany in an ever changing parade, it has not looked good at all.

We have missed our chance in Germany because the human element in our information effort has been so disappointingly inadequate. We have quartered upon Germany, as reorientation leaders, a fuzzy crew of second teamers. Germany, with its importance to the future, needed Americans of imagination and vision. Instead we have sent it leaders who were thinking principally in terms of the luxurious housing at Bad Godesberg, of the kowtowing of local servants, of the overseas pay extras and the perquisites.

Germany, since 1948, has made a miraculous recovery, but only too often it has been in spite of, not on account of, the inglorious instructors in democracy whom we have sent to counsel her.

13

Asia—Our Tragic Failure

France, which has long celebrated July 14 as its day of glory, now has another date, July 20, 1954, to remember. But it is doubtful if it will be celebrated by breaking the heads of the wine barrels and dancing in the street. Premier Mendès-France, pledged to win a truce by midnight, in the six-and-one-half years of hopeless war in Indo-China, signed the tragic papers that sold 20 million people into slavery and opened another door to the onrushing hordes of Soviet colonizers.

The event was celebrated immediately by the Soviets and their grinning allies by a cocktail party to 500 members of the press. Vodka, champagne, even wine from China were served with the caviar and all the exotic tidbits that go with the Russian soirees. How the press men celebrated was not reported.

But in the capitals of the world there were various

shades of gloom. In London, Prime Minister Churchill congratulated Anthony Eden for his share in the sell-out. But there were some Britons, less intent on the dog races and soccer games, who remembered Munich and, of later date, England's refusal to join the United States in a Southeastern Asian pact.

Paris was glad that the war was over but uneasily conscious that what the Vietminh could do, the Moroccans might also do, and many French were unhappily adjusting themselves to a new France, without Colonial possessions. In Bonn, the Germans were glad that one problem was out of the way and the Allies could get back to the business of permitting them to raise an army.

Way off in New Delhi (not so far away as it used to be), Mr. Nehru ran true to form, sending congratulations to Molotov, Eden, Chou, and Mendès-France, not to mention Mr. Dulles of the United States. In Hanoi the populace was listless, mainly wondering when they and their families would have to move out; and how long it might be before they would have to move again. Even those who could not read realized that a new, relentless tide was rising in the world.

In Washington, President Eisenhower, addressing his weekly news conference on the following day, was saddened but not bitter. He was glad that the bloodshed was over but, he added, "there were features of the agreement that we do not like." A similar understatement was made by Secretary of State John Foster Dulles but his words were voiced behind closed doors of a committee meeting.

History did not wait on Time to place blame and assay the probable results of another clear-cut victory of the Communists. Senator William Knowland of California, then Republican majority leader of the Senate, was the real spokesman for the overwhelming majority of Americans when he declared the settlement "was one of the great Communist victories of the decade."

Every political Monday-morning quarterback and after-thinker was rushing in with his theory of what had been wrong and what had not been done that should have been done. Every editorial writer and political columnist had a field day giving his version of the cause of the debacle. This much was clear: the facts were there, confronting the world.

The seers and prophets who live in the present and judge history mainly by the terms of an American Presidential term, were inclined to think that all was over and that we stood upon the brink of the unforeseeable. Others, who have a sense of philosophy and believe with Napoleon in the theory of chance—"on account of a nail etc., a battle was lost"—were willing to wait until events had taken a breather and the badly shaken forces of democracy could re-form their lines.

How much was the United States to blame for the surrender at Geneva; or was she to blame at all? There are protagonists for both viewpoints, both voluble.

Those who believe that the United States could not have stopped the tide of Communism in the Far East, claim that the death of Colonialism has been foreseen for a long time. They assert that its beginnings go back as far as the earliest riots in India against the English; and that another era dawned for the Asiatics when India broke loose. Still another milestone was the Dutch expulsion from Indonesia. Japan, with her cry of "Asia for the Asians," supplied a ready-made, magic slogan to the races who felt they had been exploited by the whites. And all the time there were the strategists of the Communist high command who were nurtured on the credo of Lenin, the master—"The way to the conquest of Paris is through Peking." The long-range viewers then, are convinced that there was little we could have done, short of a third world war, to stop the tide engulfing the Far East.

On the other side there are those, as firm in their faith as the philosophical ones, who believe that we have an historic duty to step in and arrange things according to our own concepts. These of the strong-man faith are not bothered by the cries of those who said: "We will not send our boys into the rice paddies and the jungles of the East." They are not appalled by the $3 billion worth of material we sent to bolster the failing French; they thought that we should have gone all-out, even to the H-Bomb. They are not concerned with the fact that we have prided ourselves on a policy of anti-colonialism because our own nation was born out of a revolt against British colonialism. They feel that circumstances alter cases and that the upsurge of Communism requires that we take a new look at a policy that has led us to this debacle.

There is one fact that seems insurmountable: the French lost a war because they did not have the full support of the peoples they were trying to keep free of the Communist yoke. The South Asiatics had been sold on the idea that people of their own color, even if Communists, held out greater promise to them than did their previous masters.

Another fact that cannot be brushed under the diplomatic carpet is that we, as a nation, have had no clear-cut policy as to our aims or intentions in Asia. Unfortunately, our State Department does not have continuity of foreign policy, as the British have, but must follow the political winds of changing administrations. It even has to follow the vagaries of rapidly changing expressed policies, as has happened during the past year within one administration: "Strike back with massive retaliation," a stirring war cry for one whole week. "Withdraw from the negotiations at Geneva," a policy for the next fortnight. "We will not send our troops into Indo-China." And, later: further aggression by the Communists "will be viewed by us as a matter of grave concern." That ought to scare them. But does it?

Let us consider the factors that led up to the debacle at Geneva and face frankly our share in having caused the tragedy to happen.

If there is one spot in the world where our information program should have paid off richly, it is Asia. We have been beaming propaganda to Asia's millions since 1941. We have spent literally hundreds of millions of dollars directly and indirectly on a series of information projects. OWI, USIS, AFRS, Radio Free Asia, ECA, TCA, and now USIA have swiftly followed one another, each seeking to win the Asiatic mind. All have miserably failed.

Today, Eastern Asia, aside from a few islands of American semi-control—Japan, Formosa and the Philippines —is almost a closed continent to American influence. We have not won Asiatic friendship through our sleek, streamlined propaganda plays; we have acquired smoldering, unappeasable Asiatic hate. Through vast stretches of the Asiatic continent, the United States today has scarcely an admitted friend.

Returning American visitors to the Far East during the last year bring back a harrowing report of the ill-concealed detestation of Americans, and enjoyment of our discomforture which they met on all sides among Asiatics. It is a sentiment which is not confined to Communist countries.

One of the seedbeds of anti-Americanism in Asia is democratic India. India's dislike of the United States has been shown during the past year, not only in its neutralist policy in the Korean and Indo-Chinese wars but (1) in its spurning of offered American military aid to balance our assistance of Pakistan; (2) its demand that American observers be expelled from the UN cease-fire team in Kashmir, and its refusal of visas to American officers sent as replacements; (3) its harassment of American missionaries to specified parts of India; (4) its embargo on shipment to the United States of monazite, needed by us in the production of atomic energy; (5) its insulting discharge of American technicians working on the Bakra Dam project in Punjab; (6) its refusal to permit American planes bound for Indo-China to fly over India.

These acts reflect a deepening hostility to America which cuts the American onlooker like a knife. They come despite American gifts to India since 1951 of $188,000,000, plus a loan of $190,000,000 for wheat shipments—contributions which will be swollen by $104,000,000 more in the 1955 FOA budget.

In Burma and in Indonesia the hostility is just as pronounced. Burma, after receiving $31,000,000 in American aid, closed the door to further American MSA assistance in 1953. Indonesia, which had been a beneficiary of American funds to the tune of $150,000,-000, forced the withdrawal of America's MSA mission and its replacement by the TCA. None of these countries is Communist; in none of them has the population been subjected to the anti-American brain-washing made famous by China's Reds. And yet their dislike of the United States is a consuming popular emotion.

The fade-out of America in Asia has not resulted from any dearth of American counter-efforts. The United States has been a tireless propagandist in the Asia field. It is simply that American programs have been conceived and executed without sympathy and without political intelligence.

The Office of War Information made its appearance in China in force shortly after its creation in America. Throughout the war it poured a constant stream of anti-Japanese propaganda throughout East Asia. But it also made the ineffable mistake of leaping into the middle of the vicious pro-Chinese Communist and anti-Chiang Kai-shek smear campaign of the late war years.

OWI higher ranks in the Far East included men who were later accused before the McCarran Committee of being sympathetic with Communist objectives in China. Owen Lattimore was Pacific Area Director of OWI. William L. Holland was Deputy Director of OWI. John King Fairbank was OWI Director for China.

When the war ended and some of the activities of the parent organization were handed over to the new USIS, Holland and Fairbank were the first executives of the

USIS in China and had the task of setting up the organization. The staff members whom they appointed remained as the key officers of USIS until the fall of China in 1949. Under their impulsion, USIS followed a confused, anti-Chiang Kai-shek course during the decisive years when the Communists were fighting for power. Instead of having the political intelligence to strengthen American Far East influence by vigorously supporting Asiatics like Chiang Kai-shek, who showed friendly inclinations, USIS went all-out to undermine Chiang and to build a favorable picture of the Communist Mao Tse-tung in American eyes.

The bias of USIS was so pronounced that in late 1947, *Time* magazine felt constrained to publish a breakdown of the reprints of American press comments on China which USIS had circulated in China under the directorship of W. Bradley Connors, a Fairbank appointee. The breakdown showed that anti-Chiang comments were reproduced by USIS and circulated in China in a ratio of two to one over pro-Chiang articles.

The loss of 460,000,000 Chinese to the Free World, and the unhinging of the whole American position was the inevitable consequence of the muddled American policies in China between 1945 and 1949, beginning with the blundering Marshall Mission and ending with the Dean Acheson "let the dust settle" declaration.

Through this wobbling American course, our information agencies were consistently on the wrong side. They contributed to the State Department blindness in Washington by sending biased and one-sided reports about the National Government and President Chiang. They intensified the confusion of American officials in

China by not fully emphasizing (if they were capable of assaying the situation) the historic importance to America of the advance of Communism in China.

It is obvious that American information officials who did not even understand what was happening around them had little chance to make a favorable impact upon the East Asiatic mind. They operated in a void of unreality.

USIS lost its last actual opportunity to help keep pro-American Asiatics on top when it joined the anti-Chiang Kai-shek lynching party in China in the late forties. All that it has done since has been to endeavor to pick up the pieces from this irretrievable blunder. USIA, VOA, TCA, Educational Exchange, ECA and MSA have operated vigorously in East Asia since the Communist victory of 1949 but their fight has been a losing and a rear-guard one. While they have gone through the motions of frantic propaganda, the Asiatics have slipped away before their eyes either to neutralism or to pro-Communism.

A striking example of the ineptness of some of those who have master minded our propaganda in Asia was brought to American attention by one of the Chinese Communist defectors who toured the United States after the Korea Armistice. He told of American-prepared leaflets dropped by our planes behind the Communist lines in 1951. The leaflets contained pleas to the North Korean and Chinese soldiers to lay down their arms and go home. They were captioned, "Your family is waiting back home for you."

Unfortunately, the art work on the leaflet defeated the text. Over the caption was the picture of an expen-

sive house, a well-dressed wife and a car parked beside
the door. To the Koreans and Chinese who picked it up,
the leaflet simply didn't make sense. "Home" to them
usually meant a mat-shed, or a rude one-room shelter in
the rice paddies; a private automobile was outside
their world. The psychological warriors were blunder-
ingly using Western stereotypes for Eastern minds.

In retrospect, it is now easy to perceive that our information and aid agencies have never understood the
task of combating Communism in East Asia. Two main
points of view have guided post-war Americans in Asia.
Both have been dangerously wrong.

The first is the do-gooder point of view which has
conceived of the Asia job as one of bringing sanitation,
good diet, American technical skills, and, particularly,
American democracy to East Asians. The earliest expo-
nent of this school was the forgotten Henry A. Wallace.
Its present loudest voice is that of Chester Bowles,
Truman Ambassador to India. Mr. Bowles would have
drenched the Indians with American generosity. He
proposed in 1952 that we award a billion-dollar relief
program to India, spaced out over four years, to finance
Nehru's Five Year Plan. Trusting in Nehru's good faith
with the United States, Bowles would build an American Asiatic policy on the weak reed of a quixotic Neh-
ruism.

Bowles's trustful proposals were knocked into a cocked
hat by Congress, and Bowles himself soon made his de-
parture, but the mawkish, over-sentimental attitude
which he symbolizes is still widespread among American information, aid and TCA workers in Asia. Not understanding the Asiatic mind, such do-gooders imagine

that a weak American humanitarianism can stand up against the magnetic promise of "Asia for the Asiatics" which the Communists have shrewdly inherited from the war-time Japanese. All that the Bowleses accomplish is a complete loss of face by Americans among Asiatics. The post-war Asiatic is not receptive to "Big Brothers" from the West. He wants to expel the West and do the reforming, if he does it, in his own way and time.

The second American approach which has been tried, and which has failed in Asia, is the "buy friendship" approach. Those who follow this line are not ideologues like the Bowleses, but they are equally mistaken. Their method is that of the political broker. They hope to exchange so many American millions (or billions) for a corresponding reward of Asiatic goodwill. Most of the MSA disbursement functionaries are of this mind.

Harold Stassen has now revealed that the Administration has decided to place all its chips in the Far East upon this bankrupt "buy friends" policy.

In a full-dress news conference on November 22, 1954, Mr. Stassen impressively announced that a new Marshall Plan for Asia was to be the next major undertaking of the Administration.

No figures were mentioned, but Mr. Roscoe Drummond, New York *Herald Tribune* syndicated columnist, who is close to the White House, tossed out the surmise that America's share of the cost of the new program will be close to three billion dollars a year. Mr. Drummond went on to announce that Stassen has already begun to lay the groundwork and to prepare to "soften up" the Congress to accept this huge new boondoggle.

The viciousness of this new proposal is that it contradicts President Eisenhower's own words, in his speech before the nation's editors on June 23, 1954, when the President declared that "you cannot keep any other country in the world free merely by money." The President wisely added on this occasion that "you can't buy or import a heart or a soul, or a determination to remain free."

And yet, Mr. Stassen has officially announced that the Administration has decided to go all-out for a program which, not many months ago, the President himself declared to be impossible.

Anyone even remotely familiar with Asiatic realities realizes the ineffable folly of such a project. The three billion dollars will simply go down the drain. Asia will avidly take the money but, for the most part, will remain neutralist toward primary American objectives in the West Pacific.

In Asia, as in Europe, American billions can't buy Allies.

An even more discouraging fact in the contemporary Asia situation is that many Asiatics are cynically exploiting American political gullibility to siphon additional American dollars into their economies. On top of the outright American grants, contemptuous Asiatics have discovered numerous ways of raising the ante.

One of these ways is by rigged exchange rates. For instance, in 1954, the Japanese yen was pegged at 540 to U.S. $1. This put Japanese domestic prices at least 20 to 30 per cent above world prices. The practical effect of this was to penalize exports and subsidize imports, making the Japanese economy permanently dependent upon the bounty of the United States. The same situation more or less exists in the Philippines, Formosa and South Korea.

Other ways of attracting additional American dollars are by offshore procurement, hire of local labor, loan (without stipulation of return) of American military supplies, and unilateral tariff imposts.

The whole slack system of American foreign aid encourages this situation of permanent pauperization of our Asiatic satellites. Its long-range effect is to mulct the American taxpayer for non-stop benefactions, while earning the whole-hearted contempt of the Asians whom we purportedly aid.

An amazing instance of Administration irresponsibility in dealing with our Asiatic friends was recently given in South Korea.

Although American officials in Seoul were concurrently engaged in a heated dispute with South Korean officials over the exchange rate of the Korean *hwan,* and 100,000 civilian employees of the United States had been unpaid for weeks owing to the freezing of all UN Command *hwan* accounts in Korean banks, Syngman Rhee was given an additional $100,000,000 of new American money, with no attached conditions.

So eager was FOA Director Stassen to hurry the giving of this money to Korea, while the dispute was still raging, that he made a trip to the summer White House in Denver for the sole purpose of obtaining special authorization from the President for the supplemental give-away to Korea. He got it. Syngman Rhee got the money but the Koreans did not unfreeze the *hwan* in their banks. In the end we were forced to meet our large payroll in Korea with American dollars, and the Korean Government bitterly criticized us for meeting our payrolls *in Korea!*

Syngman Rhee has been a faithful ally of the United States in our shooting war in Korea, but he does not see eye-to-eye with Washington on post-war Far Eastern policy. This incident shows how the United States loses the respect even of a friendly ally, and it plainly points up the reasons why we continually fail to get the support of larger and more important nations in other pressing world situations. Again, money is not enough!

The United States is simply making itself ridiculous by all these backings and fillings.

Late in 1954 a new agreement was announced in Washington. It settled the dispute between the South Korean and United States governments. Cost, to the American taxpayers, for the ensuing twelve months— $700,000,000!

The only American method which has a ghost of a chance of winning Asiatics, according to one school of thought, is the one worked out by General Douglas MacArthur in Japan during the years of his Supreme Command. It is the method of controlled, even-handed power. It is the method of gradualistic betterment of social and economic conditions balanced by a scrupulous respect for Asiatic sensibilities and folkways. It is the method of undeviating support of America's Asiatic friends and ruthless firmness in dealing with America's enemies or challengers. It is the method of the all-out, instead of the method of the half-hearted. It is a method, however, that would require the consent of Congress, backed by the majority of American opinion; a method that heretofore in our history we have not looked upon with favor.

Asiatics instinctively respect power. They respect

realistic, practical approaches by the West. They have no hooks in their minds upon which to hang the mealy-mouthed preachments of the "One World" impossibilists whom we have sent among them. With their rooted traditions, they can have nothing but contempt for a Washington which fires a Douglas MacArthur and sends them a Chester Bowles and a Frank P. Graham.

America lost the first trick in the battle for the Far Eastern mind when it deserted its staunchest friend, Chiang Kai-shek, in his hour of need and let him go under. It lost the second trick when it refused to fight a winning war in Korea and allowed Mao Tse-tung to escape the annihilation which we could have visited upon him in 1951. It has now lost the third trick in Indo-China, where the strong Dulles and Eisenhower words of April and May are being shamefacedly eaten in Washington as we rubber-stamp the Mendès-France summer surrender.

American information spokesmen and FOA fund-dispensers, even if they were intelligent, could not sell such a bill of goods to the Asiatic mind. But they are not intelligent. As American folly is piled upon folly in East Asia, Communist China easily rides the wave of a hypnotic anti-colonialism.

America has the power, but some failure of will stops it from exercising that power in the psychological moments when it could enforce its objectives. With the steady onrush of the Soviets, America's opportunities are narrowing. Possibly the usual American method of using words and dollars is nearing its inevitable and ineffectual conclusion.

14

Can We Afford Global Give-aways?

Were the United States endowed with limitless resources, like new Monte Cristos, we might afford the
luxury of underwriting distress throughout the world.
The seven per cent of the world's population in
America might be able to prop up the remaining ninety-
three per cent, or such portions thereof as live outside
the Iron Curtain.

Unfortunately there are sharp and painful limits to
what we can do for the rest of the world without hurting
ourselves. Those limits are already alarmingly in sight.

General Douglas MacArthur put his finger unerringly
upon this problem when he said:

"This nation's material wealth is built upon the vision
and courage, the sweat and toil, hope and faith of our
people. There has been no magic involved upon which we

might again call to replenish our denuded coffers. We can either advance upon the security of sound principles or we can plunge on to the precipice of disaster toward which we are now headed in the dangerous illusion that our wealth is inexhaustible—and can therefore be limitlessly shared with others."

A few wise voices have long been warning the American people that we are fast exhausting our patrimony. The tremendous outgo of American minerals, lumber, foodstuffs and finished products in two successive world wars has torn vast holes in our irreplaceable natural capital. We have been engaged in a non-stop performance of self-impoverishment in the Korean war and in all the give-away ECA, MSA and FOA programs through which we are asked to subsidize foreign nations. We are pursuing tariff policies, under UN and Allied pressure, which are accelerating this squander policy. Unless America cries a halt to give-aways which are not based upon a painstaking and conscientious survey of our capacity to pay, even our own magnificent economy will be seriously hurt.

One of the goosefleshy subjects of speculation by farsighted business executives is the possible exhaustion of our great mineral and oil resources. Some industries—iron ore, copper, petroleum, coal—have already approached the famine stage in some primary fields after their years of feast. The Mesabi iron range, the rich Butte and Calumet copper mines, the exhausted oil fields of Pennsylvania and Oklahoma and the dying anthracite coal regions of Pennsylvania are warning indications that our economy can wear out. Already we are near the end of our supply of lead and zinc. We supply only a trickle of our needs of tin and nickel. Our once seemingly exhaustless timber resources have shrunk from 460,000,000 acres, when the first European settlements were made, to less than 100,000,000 remaining virgin acres, mostly in the Northwest.

In agriculture the story is the same. Our founding fathers acquired a country richly endowed with an almost untouched topsoil which nature had been building steadily for a million years. In a few short generations, our wasteful, forced agricultural methods have mined away much of this topsoil and left wide stretches of our countryside denuded and infertile. Recurrent dust storms have accelerated the rate of exhaustion. When our headline-hunting politicos talk soberly about feeding the substandard world by shipping abroad America's farm surplus in great give-away programs, they are inviting a further forcing of the American soil. The danger point is still far ahead, but it exists. A responsible American leadership would dispassionately weigh the cost in soil depletion of the proposed give-away programs beffore they give the spenders *carte blanche*.

There is no imminent danger that the United States will become a have-not nation. But there is a very real danger that a continuance of the reckless, uncalculating scattering of our irreplaceable natural resources will bring a dangerous disbalance in our economy within a comparatively few years.

The question of whether we can afford the lavish aid programs that Mr. Stassen and his merry men are pressing is the great unanswered inquiry of the whole aid undertaking.

If it were true that we had overcome all of our own

domestic wants and shortages, the case for the give-aways would be more acceptable. But we have not. Although we are now living in one of the fat periods of our national career, there are great arrearages in our economy. In terms of living standards, there are yawning gaps which need to be closed. In terms of overdue and needed public works, there are scores of primary projects which have been deferred for lack of government financing. In terms of cultural goals, there are millions of Americans who are still in substandard backwardness. Before we take upon our shoulders the economic burdens of the outside world, is it unreasonable to ask that we should look after our own?

Take the question of public works. Whether our approach be that of public or private initiative, it will be agreed that there are long needed and deferred water power projects on the nation's books which have been postponed for reasons of economy. When American citizens contemplate the $99,000,000 which the United States was asked to put up in fiscal 1955 for supplies and equipment for the Ganges River reclamation project in neutralist India, plus $5,196,000 for technicians and trainees, our own deferred public works projects loom large in the imagination.

For reasons of economy the present Administration made the decision to place the Hell's Canyon Dam proposal in moth balls, and to authorize going ahead with a much smaller private project on the Snake River.

A project which has been kicking around Washington now for several years, but which has never gotten anywhere for lack of money, is the proposed Missouri Valley Authority—a plan for flood control, navigation, irrigation and power on this unruly river system. The project became snarled in Truman politics and is today probably a dead issue. And yet it remains one of the postponed and desired public works proposals which, in its original or different form, could yield rich returns in human values to the millions of Americans in the Missouri Valley. But while MVA remains only a plan, International Development engineers are drafting programs of similar scope for Asia and the Near East to be financed by American handouts.

What has become of the Seven-Year Straus Reclamation Plan which was proposed for the years 1948-54? The Plan is buried hell-deep, and Michael W. Straus, its author, is one of the forgotten men of Washington; but to many Americans in the affected regions it has reality.

The Seven Year Plan would have created 24,000 new family-size irrigation farms from present waste spots, but it would have cost $3,891,900,000. The amount is a formidable one, but it compares with the more than $16,000,000,000 that the United States poured out in foreign aid during the same years, 1948-52, through ECA and MSA. Had we bought the Straus Plan, at least we would have had the public works, whereas the $16,000,000,000 is lost irretrievably.

Although all three of these cited projects were objected to because of the Socialistic form in which they were presented, there can be no questioning the fact that the plans themselves had sound merit. Taking the Socialism out of them would have been a matter of detail. But all three were tabled because "we didn't have the money."

The 83rd Congress, after much goading by the States,

appropriated $900,000,000 for highway building, a mere bagatelle, by foreign aid standards. But President Eisenhower, in his message to the Conference of Governors on July 12, 1954, admitted that the nation badly needed a highway-building program totalling $50,-000,000,000. This is the conceded arrearage of the nation in the single basic item of transportation.

Our prodigal generosity in foreign aid takes on an even more questionable light when we contemplate the stark failure of Washington to make the United States self-sufficient.

One of the spurious arguments for foreign programs is the contention that we must keep backward nations out of Communist hands because they are producers of raw materials which are essential to our economy. Thus we must get rubber from Malaya, uranium from the Congo, manganese and chromite from South Africa and the Gold Coast, etc. Because America, for all its bounteous natural resources, is not economically self-sufficient, it is argued with some cogency that the perimeter of our defense is in Southeast Asia, in the Near East, in tropical Africa. To secure that perimeter, we must pour out our weary billions.

The fact that is overlooked in such discussion is that the billions, or a relatively small part of them, could be better employed developing self-sufficiency in this hemisphere.

In the case of uranium, for instance, instead of fatalistically accepting the fact that we must depend upon open sea lanes to bring our uranium from Central Africa, a better use of our money would be to finance exploration and prospecting for uranium deposits in the

United States and in the wide stretches of Canada and South America. In the case of manganese, a "must" metal, the answer is to be found in the development of our high cost manganese fields in New Mexico.

The challenging importance of this problem was recently pointed out in the report of the Malone Committee on America's resources in this hemisphere for the 77 minerals and materials which the Committee lists as essential to our economy and our preparedness to wage war. The Committee declared that:

"During the last two decades established procurement practices have dangerously increased our dependence upon nations across major oceans for the critical materials without which this Nation cannot survive. Evidence is conclusive that we have become dependent upon overseas suppliers across such major oceans for many of such critical materials. We must avoid dependence upon an overseas supplier to the extent that he could suddenly render us impotent by withdrawing supplies of critical materials during a world conflict, or could use such dependence as a political or economic bargaining lever."

Instead of exploring the avenues of self-sufficiency, the policy makers in Washington have chosen to take resort in stockpiling. By an act of Congress in 1946, the Munitions Board of the Department of Defense was charged with accumulating strategic commodities necessary in war, on a five-year basis, and a huge amount of defense funds was allocated to this purpose.

However, by some curious working of the bureaucratic mind, the State Department, instead of making the United States independent of other countries in the necessary commodities, thwarted the purpose of the stockpiling program in 1951 by enrolling the United States in an extra-legal body, the International Materials Conference, which proceeded to set quotas of strategic commodities for each member nation. Since the United States had only one vote among the 28 members (which includes several neutralist powers), this was equivalent to placing American stockpiling policies at the mercy of 27 other countries. While it lasted, IMC actually assumed the authority to rule whether stockpiling would be approved in the case of particularly scarce commodities.

But the real *reductio ad absurdum* of the whole stockpiling program is seen in the fact that, when European countries themselves began to stockpile under the IMC rules, it was America's ECA which loaned them money to purchase commodities. Thus, we were placing ourselves in the grotesque position, through ECA, of financing other nations to compete with us in the acquisition of the scarce commodities which we needed for our own safety. The stockpiling policy, under these conditions, has become one of the most disappointing American experiments of the Cold War. It has never even approached its goals.

All the billions which we have scattered about the world since 1947 have failed to give the United States the most important security of all—the security which comes from self-sufficiency.

While we were floundering in such profitless experiments as IMC, Washington's shortsightedness permitted one of our basic strategic industries, coal, to languish. In our willingness to aid foreign industries, tariff rates on imports of foreign residual oil, competing with coal, have been placed so low that oil imports have more than trebled since 1946. The consequence is that coal markets have fallen off so sharply that American coal miners have lost the equivalent of 23,000 jobs.

When both coal operators and the United Mine Workers petitioned for government action in this situation, Mr. Stassen, on August 5, 1954, came up with a pre-election announcement that the FOA planned to purchase ten million tons of coal in fiscal 1955 to be sent to aided countries. In order to get the maximum political effect from his announcement, he repeated it again in Denver on September 21, specifying States where coal was to be bought.

So far from easing the coal situation, the *United Mine Workers Journal* described the actual effects of the Stassen announcements as follows:

"Reports from coal export circles are that foreign purchases of coal in commercial channels have virtually stopped since the Stassen announcement, as foreign buyers are bewildered and do not know whether to continue placing orders in regular channels or to look to the U. S. Government program. Another important effect of the Stassen announcement has been to cause an increase in ocean freight rates. . . . Thus, Stassen's only contribution is confusion and stopping even what small export trade the coal industry did have.

"Coal operator circles are also skeptical and are awaiting clarification of the program before they throw their hats in the air over a marginal operation which at best would offer only an additional week's running time spread out over a year. Unless it were all concentrated in one area, it would hardly be noticed, they point out."

The *Journal* made the acute observation on Mr. Stassen's press agentry that "it has sometimes been observed that he who talks the most actually mines the least coal."

Although help to our domestic coal industry has lagged, in another field the FOA has acted with sure-footed speed. This was in its aid program to European coal operators. While American coal miners were petitioning for action, FOA rushed through a loan of $100,-000,000 of American money to the European Coal and Steel Community to strengthen the principal European competitor of the United States coal industry. It was an arresting example of the Europe-mindedness of so many of our present Washington statesmen.

Even if America is spared from the awful test of a third World War, the empty security which our foreign aid billions purchase for us is won at the expense of the basic living standards of the American people.

There are appalling economic and cultural lags in our national life which the billions which have gone to our "Allies" could have relieved. It has been estimated that a ten per cent increase in American production, if distributed equitably, would give every American family a comfortable and adequate standard of living. Our production indices steadily rise, but the increment goes in large part to our never-ending foreign give-aways and to our mostly worthless propaganda boondoggling.

Is it not time for an American statesmanship to emerge which will make the welfare of our own people the overshadowing aim of national policy?

One need not be a statistician to recognize the vastness of the unfinished tasks in America which would give

Americans a decent standard of life. We have spent billions on slum clearance and home building in our cities in the last fifteen years, but we have only scratched the surface. In every American city there is a steady and losing battle between slum clearance and deterioration. Meanwhile, millions of Americans are doomed to live in substandard and unsanitary dwellings and tenements because there isn't enough money to make an all-out attack on the slum. The same 83rd Congress which voted to give Mr. Stassen $3,368,800,000 for foreign aid found it necessary, for economy's sake, to cut down the Administration's request for a housing bill which would yield 140,000 new housing units during the next five years. And the problem of rural housing, which is even more challenging than the urban, is almost completely ignored.

Our educational plant is bursting at the seams as an increasing child population outstrips our existing facilities. All over the country schools are resorting to the two-platoon system to avoid overcrowded classes, with resultant shortening of instruction periods. As Walter Lippmann recently wrote:

"The level of education is falling because our schools, lacking adequate resources, are being compelled to depreciate the quality of their teaching. They are being compelled to teach less to more and more pupils. The tragic consequence is that the gifted children—from whom must come the leaders and the teachers and the discoverers—are not being given adequate opportunities."

Plain lack of money to keep our school plants up to date is drying up the well springs of our nation's culture. It is lowering the norm of our citizenship.

Similarly, in the public health field, we have staggering tasks to accomplish. Hospital facilities, including
clinics for the low-income population, are falling far behind our needs. Medical costs are rising precipitously.
Medical research, despite the distinguished work of
some of our foundations, is retarded in many instances
for lack of endowment. The shortage of nurses and laboratory technicians is steadily widening.

And yet, with our own population still handicapped
with ill health which better facilities could mitigate or
prevent, the United States, in the last seven years, has
found $97,231,000 to contribute to the United Nations'
Children's Fund for child health overseas. We have been
able to send teams of American public health technicians to India, Iran, Egypt and other countries from
FOA funds. We have been able to contribute a large
quota of the annual budget of the World Health Organization of the United Nations. The motive of all these
benefactions is laudable, but low-income Americans
may well ask the question, can we afford it?

An inventory of our national needs discloses wide
ranging tasks, in all social fields, which have been
deferred for lack of financing. International-minded
Americans who weep over the sufferings of the teeming
millions of Asia and Africa should be reminded of the
old truism that charity begins at home.

The question of whether we can afford the foreign
aid billions is not an academic one to the American people. Wage-earning and small-salaried Americans who
see one-fourth of their meager incomes snatched away
for the Federal income tax realize sadly that everybody
pays. When we confront a situation where it costs us

$8,000,000,000 a year just to pay interest on the accumulated national debt, the proposal that we pour out additional billions to aid our "Allies" affronts our every sense of prudence and governmental responsibility.

Wise Herbert Hoover pointed out in his 1954 speech to the American Society of Newspaper Editors that a further bitter cost to the American people of our reckless government spendings has been creeping inflation. The deficit borrowing of the last 23 years, he declared, has reduced the purchasing power of the American dollar by 80 per cent. This represents, he pointed out, a staggering loss to the many millions of Americans who hold insurance policies, bank savings, bonds, pensions, or other fixed assets. Thus the bite which the tax collector takes out of the ordinary American citizen when he taxes him on April 15 for Mr. Stassen's and Mr. Streibert's boondogglings is cruelly increased by the further cost to the taxpayer from the shrinkage of his savings and investments, as the dollar plummets. This is the ugly side of the pink colored "Quart of Milk a day for every Hottentot" program which is seldom contemplated by the heedless Washington billion-spenders.

Some time the givings must stop, if we are to escape national financial disaster. The time to stop them is now, and not in some vague tomorrow.

15

Are Our Ambassadors Becoming Robots?

One of the unhappy effects of the weedy growth of our foreign aid and information agencies abroad has been the decline of our Ambassadors. With so many eager-beavers moving about throughout the world, with Presidential sub-authority, defining American foreign policy, our regular diplomatic channels have gone into a sad, steady decline.

No one has planned it this way, but the condition has grown up as an inevitable result of the emergency character of the aid and information programs. Each program, when it has been launched, has started out as a purely temporary experiment, tagged with a definite expiration date. The dislocations which it might bring to our permanent diplomatic machinery have not been feared because its life has been expected to be so brief.

But none of the newcomers died. Inevitably when

the expiration date arrives, there is always the "emergency" excuse for another extension. If there is public resistance to the extension, the fond legislative parents simply repackage the agency. OWI becomes USIS, and then IIA and finally USIA. OSS becomes CIA. ECA becomes MSA and then FOA. The Fulbright Act becomes Educational Exchange Service. But they never terminate. There are always new and bigger "emergencies" to justify their continuance and proliferation.

As a result, in an era when America faces crushing international responsibilities, our diplomatic establishments abroad are a tangle of conflicting authority. Not one but several voices define American foreign policy in the major capitals overseas. In Paris, until recently, there were actually four permanently established American officials who had the rank of Ambassador. Our accredited State Department diplomat in France was, under such circumstances, but one of a quadrumvirate. FOA, USIA and HICOG officials, each reporting to a different chief in Washington, roam Europe and interpret American policy to the bemused European chancelleries.

In Washington, this problem of divided diplomatic authority is studiously ignored by an administration which is self-dedicated to governmental efficiency. The diplomatic mess abroad has not improved under the Eisenhower Administration. With the prestige of the State Department eroded by the McCarran Committee revelations of its colossal blunders in China, "Foggy Bottom" had few friends when the Eisenhower reorganizers commenced to strip it of its functions.

Under this administration, the incredible action has

been taken of setting up three major-rank independent establishments dealing with foreign policy, each autonomous from the Department of State.

The United States Information Agency was created as an independent establishment to administer agencies which have always hitherto been divisions of the State Department. The United States Information Center Service, the International Education Exchange Service, the International Broadcasting Service (Voice of America), the International Press Service, and the International Motion Picture Service—the five new major divisions of USIA—were all located in the State Department prior to the President's Reorganization Plan No. 8, effective August 1, 1953. Then their activities could be subordinated to State Department policies. Now USIA enjoys an ambiguous autonomy, subject to consultation with the Secretary of State, and reporting to the President through the National Security Council. Actually, for all practical purposes, the propaganda Director runs his own show.

Similarly, the independent status of the Mutual Security Administration, which stemmed from the controversial 1948 decision to divorce the Marshall Plan from the State Department, was prolonged in 1953 by the President's Reorganization Plan No. 7. MSA was broadened into Foreign Operations Administration, and Technical Cooperation Administration (Point 4) was detached from the State Department and placed under its rule.

A third independent body, with agents operating throughout the world, is Central Intelligence Agency, which President Eisenhower inherited from the preceding administration. Formerly under the jurisdiction of the Department of Defense, CIA now enjoys a completely autonomous status, reporting only to the President. Even its budget is exempt from Congressional approval and review, and is allotted by the President from special funds.

In Europe and other overseas posts, American Ambassadors face the difficult task of working with representatives from all three of these powerful independent agencies, none of them subject to State Department discipline or direct control. Each, by his very functions, is continually making impact upon the execution of American policy abroad. He is interpreting that policy to foreigners. But he works on lines of authority which constantly bypass the State Department, and its Ambassador. If the FOA or USIA or CIA representative is cooperative and a "team" man, no serious differences of policy will usually arise between himself and the Ambassador. But it is the officious, self-important ass, clothed for the first time in his dreary life with governmental authority, who makes trouble for the State Department.

Such bulls-in-the-china-shop—and the foreign service seems to attract a disproportionate number of them— make a bad joke of American prestige abroad. And under the present set-up, the Ambassadors possess only indirect ways of disciplining them. Ostensibly, under the Eisenhower reorganizations, the independent agency men are expected to clear their policy-effecting activities through a secretary in the Embassy. Actually, it doesn't work that way at all.

A further factor which weakens the Ambassador's position is money. The major American spendings abroad now don't pass through his hands. The foreigners with whom he must deal as an Ambassador realize that somebody else, reporting to a Stassen or a Streibert in Washington, has the final voice in the eagerly sought American hand-outs or services. It is inescapable that the independent agency man, with his power of purse, often overtops the Ambassador, in his day-to-day relations with foreign officials.

The financial advantage that the independents enjoy, in comparison with the regular diplomatic establishment, may be seen by comparison of over-all budgets. Thus, the FOA, for 1955, will operate on a budget of $5,243,575,979. USIA will have a budget of more than $77,000,000. But for all the activities of the Department of State, the total appropriated budget is only $108,-000,000.

A striking example of the advantage which USIA enjoys over the State Department in international situations occurred in Geneva. At this epochal conference, where the State Department faced the prospect of making international decisions which would determine the whole future direction of the United States, a single State Department representative, Henry Suydam, was present to interpret the American position to the press. In contrast to this, USIA sent a whole battery of newsmen, radio men, cameramen, photographers and liaison men to cover the conference. It is a tribute to the superior ability of the State Department over that of the independent agencies to handle a delicate diplomatic situation that it was Suydam, and not the USIA mob, to whom the world press representatives crowded to get their answers.

It must be admitted, however, that the administrative mix-up in American foreign relations is not the only reason for the declining prestige of American diplomacy in recent years. The increasing disposition of Washington to use our principal embassies as rewards for unqualified political supporters has hurt the State Department. Men whose only apparent qualification is that they were "for Ike before Chicago" now represent the United States in some of the top posts abroad. Lacking the background and instinctive sureness which makes a great ambassador, they have given the United States weak representation during the post-war years. On their own team they have shown themselves, in frequent instances, to be no match for the White House appointed Stassen and Streibert men.

When we recall some of the great American ambassadors of yesterday, it seems inconceivable that any of them would have tolerated the humiliating division of authority which the present ambassadorial crop take uncomplainingly. Such towering names from the past as Myron T. Herrick, Charles G. Dawes, Andrew W. Mellon, Jesse Isidor Straus, James W. Gerard, Richard Washburn Child, Josephus Daniels, Henry Morgenthau, Sr., Whitelaw Reed, Henry White, and Dwight W. Morrow, as well as the names of those who have served more recently, Joseph P. Kennedy, Stanton Griffiths, Joseph C. Grew, Walter S. Gifford, and Henry P. Fletcher, occur to the mind as representatives of the best in the American diplomatic tradition. It is difficult to imagine any question of who would enunciate American policy in the embassies which they ruled.

It is a sad admission that there are no Herricks or

Kennedys or Gerards in President Eisenhower's diplomatic posts.

It is not surprising that State Department prestige declines throughout the world in an administration which has very few first-rate men in foreign diplomatic posts. The recent example of diplomatic expertness in Guatemala by the then American Ambassador John E. Peurifoy gave the American people a welcome exhibition of what American diplomacy can be when administered by professionals. But, Peurifoy belongs to an old school which, today, has few members.

We shall make little progress in overcoming the dangerously bad overseas climate of public opinion toward America until we restore the Department of State to its proper place in our American government, as the maker and interpreter of foreign policy. It is being nudged out of that place today by the outsize independent agencies which have grown up in this era of psychological warfare and "mutual security." It is complacently accepting a robot status in a situation where it should be supreme.

Not until we have a courageous refacing of the whole problem of foreign aid and information in our government and its relationship to foreign policy and the maintenance of the economic stability of the United States can we hope to remove the dangerous imbalance.

16

Propaganda Can't Win
for Americans

One of the most misleading notions that have entrapped
the official American mind since V-J Day has been the
belief that propaganda can do in peace, or even in the
Cold War, what it did in the late shooting war.

The whole rickety structure of foreign information,
into which we have poured our hundreds of millions, is
erected upon this baseless conviction. An urgent duty
of the American people is to re-examine their concepts
of propaganda, and to reassess them.

Actually, propaganda has a necessary role in war, as
both World Wars I and II demonstrated. Skillfully directed, it saves lives and shortens hostilities. It is an
agent of demoralization when turned against retreating or losing enemy troops: it is an agent of defeatism
when turned against the home front. It is in the nature
of such propaganda that it needs to have little relationship to truth: indeed, the most effective propaganda

coups in both wars have been variations of the "Big Lie" technique—the British atrocity stories and pictures in World War I, or OSS's "Operation Annie" in World War II. Such war-time stunts are feints and hoaxes, cynically designed to throw enemy troops and populations off balance.

But the fact that such operations have been sensationally effective under war conditions is no analogy for peace. In normal times the only function of a good information program is to tell the truth, not falsehood—to sell goodwill, not dissimulation. Probably the greatest mistake of our costly post-war information program has been its attempt to carry over, into peace times, the fabulous mentality of war.

Regardless of how jaundiced the reader's opinion of the man's controversial place in the world of journalism may be, the fact cannot be ignored that William Randolph Hearst knew the power of the press and how to exploit that power. He also knew the difference between fact and fiction. He wrote:

"President Roosevelt is entirely and emphatically right when he tells the conference of pressmen that propaganda should not be printed in newspapers as fact. Propaganda is not fact. It is falsehood. It is, in truth, willfully distorted out of all resemblance to truth, in the interests of one or another party to a dispute or conflict.

"Propaganda is, at best, an opinion, and opinion should not be printed as fact even if it is an honest opinion. And propaganda is neither honest fact nor honest opinion. It is essentially dishonest." *

* Quoted from *Newsmen Speak* by Edmond D. Coblentz.

The disastrous impact of current American propaganda upon traditionally friendly people abroad was strikingly pointed out to the author by a prominent French businessman and firm anti-Communist.

"The naked truth is," he declared, "that all Europeans hate propaganda in any form because they have, and for many years, been propagandized to death. They don't believe propaganda when it comes from their own government: they won't believe it from yours. Your hordes of busybody press agents in Paris and throughout France actually harm Franco-American relations, and more than you would believe."

When the present Administration assumed power, there was reason to expect a new and effective approach to the information task.

President Eisenhower, in setting up the USIA in October, 1953, specifically stated that the "new agency" would present factual reports without attempting to imprint American culture on other nations. And Theodore C. Streibert, in assuming the Directorship, defined as his intended policy: "Avoiding a propagandistic tone . . . we shall, therefore, concentrate on objective factual news reporting and appropriate commentaries."

These were reassuring intentions, but how disillusioning has been the follow-up. A few perfunctory changes involving the reshuffling of the top command. A temporary reduction of the vastly overstaffed personnel— these things were done with maximum promotional fanfare. But the vitally important transformation of the program from a vehicle of noisy and often provocative propaganda to an honest, thoughtful and intelligent presentation of America's aspirations and hopes to the world—this has not been done.

The USIA continues in its obtuse course, making enemies and critics for America instead of friends. The fine and bold resolutions of 1953 have withered away into disappointing non-fulfillment.

Our present Information Agency will never be effective for Americans because its chief operators are too busy catering to the administration which happens to be in power. They are too busy over-promoting politicians in countries where there are no votes for them. Moreover, they are too busy with never-ending campaigns for more funds to enlarge their already too big and unmanageable global establishment for press agentry. They therefore have no time to pinpoint a job of good press relations for Americans and to confine that job to the countries and places where our Government requires such efforts.

The tragedy of the situation is that what ought to be done is perfectly obvious. We are the victims of our own overorganization. We have erected a much too costly and complicated superstructure to do a job which can be done with vastly greater effectiveness by a relatively simple and inexpensive agency administered from within the Department of State.

Instead we have built, and the American taxpayer is unknowingly supporting, a cumbersome bureaucratic machine with thousands of employees constantly seeking to justify their existence with blown-up radio projects, propaganda-slanted motion pictures, ineffective and totally unneeded cabled news reports, elaborate libraries often far removed from the native population centers,

subsidized newspapers, magazines and anti-Communist
slick books and pamphlets. The books and pamphlets are
distributed almost exclusively to specialized intelligentsia groups with little or no influence at all in the countries where they reside.

Also, there are highly questionable religious "inspira-
tional" programs, synthetic propaganda for free enterprise, etc., all of which grinds on and on globally and
planlessly by sheer force of the bureaucratic pressures
behind it. In reality, we find ourselves in the unfortunate position of maintaining these ineffective and all
too often harmful promotional knick-knacks merely because we have them on our hands!

It is a tragic fact that no ruthless and thoroughgoing
overhauling of this costly and inherited apparatus has yet
been made by President Eisenhower and his advisers.

When it was pointed out to the present Administration that a whole segment of waste could be eliminated
by abolishing the $4,612,177 world-wide propaganda film
service, the President's budget estimates asked for $6,-
964,000 for fiscal 1955 to continue this ridiculous and
unnecessary program.

When, in passing the 1955 appropriation, the House
voted a cut of $8,000,000 in the over-all USIA appro-
priation, direct White House pressure caused the Senate
to add $12,000,000. Only in conference with Congress-
ional leaders was a final budget of $77,000,000 approved.
This was $20,000,000 less than the first White House de-
mand. And this was $40,000,000 more than is actually
required to pay for a properly conceived and directed
overseas information effort.

For more than twenty years during the administrations of Presidents Roosevelt, Truman and Eisenhower, the American people have been conditioned to accept government expenditures and deficits in the billions. Now, as in the past, the President and his chief spokesmen and advisers insist that only millions are spent for propaganda abroad in terms of government spending, that this is only a drop in the Atlantic Ocean. That is true, but what remains unsaid is that in terms of potential damage to our country and all our citizens, the impact of the USIA on most foreigners may, in the end, prove to be as dangerous for peace and security as the force of a Texas tornado at the height of its destructive fury.

Obviously, if every effective effort to eliminate discredited agencies and personnel dry rot is going to be met with a furious administration struggle to perpetuate them, we shall get nowhere in our endeavor to bring realism to our information program.

As the USIA official caste battles determinedly to preserve its rotten boroughs, the activities of the whole USIA apparatus are turned increasingly toward the domestic public opinion field. Instead of concentrating upon the job of winning friends for the United States abroad an enlarging proportion of their time is spent in extravagant and often untruthful claims made for the sole purpose of attempting to win support for the USIA at home. We talk to ourselves, instead of to the growingly hostile world.

If we free our minds of the special pleading of the USIA partisans, the task which needs to be done is crystal clear.

We must restore the responsibility for foreign information to the State Department where it belongs. It was a mistake of the first magnitude to set up an autonomous organization, with authority to interpret American foreign policy to other nations. That task has traditionally been located in the State Department, and in the Embassies and Legations abroad. It is a task which our Ambassadors and their assistants are peculiarly trained to perform with finesse. To set up a dual hierarchy in each capital, with authority stemming directly from Washington, to interpret American policy, is to undercut the negotiating authority of our diplomats. It is to make robots of our Ambassadors.

One immediate result of such a change could be an end to the present competitive talking. Pronouncements could be narrowed down to the one responsible spokesman and all the runners-up, with contradictory edicts and viewpoints, could be eliminated. Our Secretary of State might then find time to count ten before rushing into a torrent of words every time a red shadow crosses before his eyes.

How persistently President Eisenhower and Secretary Dulles chatter on foreign affairs is shown in the following:

Speeches Delivered Between Jan. 1953 and July 1954.

EISENHOWER	DULLES	CHURCHILL	EDEN
44	38	14	7

And, during the same period the world was reminded of the Soviet menace as follows:

EISENHOWER	DULLES	CHURCHILL	EDEN
13	26	NONE	3

Compared to the President, the voluble British Prime Minister is a Sphinx. Thinking aloud on foreign policy has proved a handicap to our foreign relations.

It would be reassuring to record that some of this marathon Presidential talking was directed toward a restatement of America's great historic traditions. The American story, told in its moving nobility, is the most powerful message that government officials and agencies can convey to a confused world. Unhappily, there is little of this saga in the utterances of our national spokesmen. The speeches are too full of other people's problems and other people's goals to get across the true dynamism of America. Even our great national anniversaries and the birthdays of the great Americans of the past are seldom honored, by our national leaders, with public discussion of America's historic meaning.

In our failure to do this, we are revealing a national inferiority complex. The real American story, of course, is deathless. It illumines the greatest pages of history. It will gain luster in the hearts of mankind, with the passage of years. But it can be blunted and obscured by "slick" American propaganda overseas, and by attempts to top the Communist "Big Lie" with a bigger one. It can be reduced to the absurd by such inane exhibitions as the new Bernays Committee.

The State Department does not need a top-heavy, highly departmentalized organization, such as the present one, to do the information job. What it needs is a qualified press officer, attached to each Embassy and Legation, working directly under the instructions of the Ambassador or Minister, with a small directing staff in

Washington. The press officer would be charged with the duty of monitoring public opinion media and influences as they affect the United States, and of taking such steps as the Ambassador deems necessary to interpret American policy favorably. In this undertaking, he would be assisted by a small staff of local newspapermen, who understand expertly the public opinion influences in their nation and the effective techniques for their guidance.

Obviously, there is nothing flashy or gadgety about such an information operation. It would not operate behind an impressive front of huge offices. But if it lacks the brass band effects of USIA, it also avoids the bull-in-the-china-shop approach which has made USIA a threat and not a spur to American goodwill abroad. It is simply the tactful application of the newspaperman's know-how to specific trouble situations in each foreign country.

Not unlike the novice duck hunter, the USIA descends, with great fanfare, upon the world scene loaded with the wrong kind of ammunition and too many kinds of it. It shoots wild at the first pigeon crossing the horizon. It scores no hits for Americans.

Certainly we need and should have a "Voice of America," but beamed only to countries where its effectiveness could be depended upon. And only in the form of a terse, strictly factual news program confined to interpreting American foreign policy and to nailing anti-American lies. To render such overseas radio service we do not need to maintain nearly 1,000 government broadcasters in Washington, D. C., alone! Instead, and to keep its contact with reality, the over-all policies and direction of the Voice might well be placed under the supervision of the major American radio and press associations.

Additionally, radio broadcasts to the satellite countries are both important and effective. Millions of people entrapped in the captive nations of Eastern Europe once enjoyed freedom and would like to have it again. This, then, is a real weakness in the Iron Curtain and one that we should constantly exploit with news broadcasts from our world, together with playbacks of news and names of people and their problems that reach the free world from these blacked-out areas.

The men in the Kremlin know that, in the event of war, the tens of millions whom they have made prisoner in the satellite nations would, at the first opportunity, turn on their captors like angry rattlesnakes. Therefore, we should never stop exploiting this, Moscow's principal weakness and constant worry. Every effort should be made to remind the Soviet of what is in store for them if they start a full-scale war.

A semi-public organization, the American Heritage Foundation, sponsor of Radio Free Europe, actually pierces these Kremlin-enslaved lands with hard-hitting broadcasts to refute Communist lies and answer threats made to a once-free people. These Radio Free Europe broadcasts have proved to be powerful weapons in bolstering the morale of seventy millions of enslaved people. Equally important, they serve to keep the Soviet oppressor off balance. However, for this activity we do not need, and should not have, two American voices broadcasting to the satellite nations. Obviously, this present duplication of effort and rivalry between the USIA and Radio

Free Europe only creates confusion in the minds of the listeners. Based upon dependable reports of long and excellent performance, this very worth-while program should be entrusted exclusively to Radio Free Europe.

The three American press associations—the Associated Press, the United Press and the International News Service—daily send many thousands of words throughout the world. This professional, unbiased and full coverage of what is happening throughout the United States every hour and every day is the best and only kind of propaganda that should be issued from a land of free people. The USIA's 6,000-word overseas news cable is a costly and totally unnecessary duplication of the services maintained by the American press associations. Our government's propaganda news cable should be taken off the backs of the American taxpayers at once.

Likewise, no other country enjoys such complete magazine and newspaper circulation throughout the world. These facilities, detailed in a previous chapter, make it all too obvious that the USIA's subsidized and slanted newspapers, slick magazines and pamphlets are, by comparison, ineffective and often annoying.

Bold claims have been made concerning the importance of our libraries, maintained in foreign countries throughout the world. But it is sheer fantasy to believe that the elaborate establishments operated by the USIA in Paris, Rome, Cairo and elsewhere are of any great value in the furtherance of American relations in these places. In too many important cities these libraries are situated in locations that are out of bounds for the native populations.

Libraries which have degenerated into mere reading

and writing rooms for American tourists should be discontinued. Also, a competent appraisal should be made of our invasion, with libraries and cultural centers, countries populated with backward people. There, at best, only a small portion of the population can possibly be influenced by the more elaborate adult presentations. No other nation attempts to compete with us in the furtherance of these government-promoted absurdities!

In the field of educational motion pictures the USIA has, for years, joyfully wasted tens of millions of dollars in unneeded film production and global circulation projects. Recently, according to reports in film trade circles, this Agency compounded its previous extravagances of producing fifty subjects annually, by adding, and all at once, several hundred more short subjects with recordings in thirty-two foreign languages!

This addition was made to an already greatly overproduced educational program, the sole value of which is to provide selected scholastic films for showing in foreign schools and colleges. For this activity Great Britain maintains a similar service on a greatly reduced scale; and the British charge for all sales and rentals of educational films furnished to foreign scholastic outfits. The funds derived from these services pay for their maintenance.

In sorry contrast, Uncle Sam first operates in the most wasteful and extravagant manner possible and then gives everything away! Moreover, the USIA's overextended backlog of already-produced films is sufficient to cover adequately the educational exhibition outlets of the entire world for years to come.

It is, therefore, all too obvious that the government

should definitely end the extravagance of producing and distributing propaganda films. This activity is indefensible; our Hollywood film industry, offering pure entertainment and not propaganda to the silver screens of the world—the theaters where the multitudes go for entertainment—has proved itself American's foremost foreign salesman—and for the past fifty years!

If proof were needed of the pathetic inadequacy of our present costly information program, the French torpedoing of the European Defense Community sharply supplies it. Perhaps nothing which we could have done in France would have averted this setback to our European program. The point is that we did not take the most obvious steps to avert it. Although our USIA establishment in Paris is princely in its scale of operations, our highly paid information officers did not sell EDC to the French people during the two years when the program was dangling in uncertainty.

Although billions of American dollars have been handed over to the French government in military and economic aid through FOA and its predecessors, no one had the elementary common sense to attach adherence to EDC as the necessary condition for the grant of the money. America, after lavish information and aid efforts in France, found itself caught flat-footed.

With our European plans bungled by the ineptitude of American confusionists in European capitals, we now learn the USIA is trumpeting a grandiose propaganda scheme for Southeast Asia and Latin America.

The swarming millions of Asia, unreachable either by the printed page or by radio, are now to become subjects for the experimentation of our USIA Psykwar experts.

Likewise, in Central and South America where the millions of poor native peoples have for years been envious and jealous of the rich North Americans, our propagandists will, by their open-handed extravagances, henceforth enlarge the ill-will of the have-not hordes in the lands south of the Border and thus actually aid Communist infiltration in this hemisphere.

As a hidden-ball trick, to get the nation's mind off the propaganda and aid debacle throughout Europe, these new concentrations are understandable. But they are not defensible in any calculus of results. USIA, which has failed miserably throughout Europe, is certainly not likely to achieve any worthwhile success in the more hazardous fields of Asia and South and Central America.

In all these regions of the world, propaganda exploiting the ideas and ideals of a favored land and people located thousands of miles away can hardly be expected to influence permanently millions of ill-fed and ill-clothed people who are concerned only with the life-long struggle to keep body and soul together.

It is high time for our Washington politicians and their deputies to understand that in their high sounding truth campaigns and their incessant demands for more billions for aid and propaganda, they are, in reality, attempting to change the living standards of most of the backward areas of the world.

Increasingly, Americans are questioning whether this global WPA and the propaganda blasts to support it can be continued without eventually wrecking the economy of the United States, which is the long expressed hope (and prediction) of the Kremlin's despots.

For these reasons the move of the USIA director in setting up a Cultural Affairs Advisership in his Office of Policy and Programs is an appalling sign of ineptitude. If present plans mature, we are to have more, not less, American breast-beating abroad.

No one has better expressed the danger of going off on this tangent than did James Ratliff, able editorial columnist of the Cincinnati *Enquirer*. He wrote:

"If there is anything more calculated to lose friends and influence people the wrong way than standing in their front yard and telling them how good YOU are, we can't imagine what it would be."

A world-wide drive, through all the outposts of the Information Service, is to be sparked, to sell the world on American culture, "including sports and political manifestations." The Advisership is headed by Dr. Joseph Canter, assisted by Dr. Guy E. Snavely, both excellent men, whose willingness to assume such a dead-end task is surprising. The bureaucratic mind which could conceive the desirability of such a program, in the present world temper, is a revealing exhibit of what is actually wrong with the USIA.

While our information experts pursue the wraith of grandiose projects, one program of trifling cost and of proven results has aroused little interest in the USIA precincts. This is the program of organized letter writing by American citizens of foreign extraction to their relatives and friends behind the Iron Curtain or in fence-sitting nations. This program was first initiated by a chain of newspapers in 1948 coincident with the Italian parliamentary elections. Its results were surprisingly good. The imaginative quality of mind which can evolve such a program is the faculty which is urgently needed in the planning of our whole information effort.

An important area in which we seem to have missed the boat is the European fair. International trade fairs, where buyers and sellers come together in great numbers, are important meeting places for Europeans from both sides of the Curtain. They are traditional marts of ideas and information, as well as goods.

Such a setting should be hand-made for American products, with their unrivalled superiority over anything that Communism has to offer. At such fairs, American industry could do a terrific selling job for American free enterprise.

Unfortunately, through lack of imagination in Washington, this opportunity has been allowed to go by default and Russia has stepped sensationally into the limelight. A painful instance was the 1954 Salonika Fair, held in a nation, Greece, which is a close ally of the United States. The Salonika Fair traditionally attracts at least 1,000,000 visitors. Russia appeared in Salonika with the largest and most imposing exhibit of manufactured goods, presided over by forty Russian technicians. So huge was the Russian showing at Salonika, according to the New York *Times,* that the machinery exhibits alone were large enough to clog three New York City blocks.

With the usual too little and too late reaction, Washington leaders are now talking about taking $5 million from the foreign aid funds to finance effective American participation in future fairs. While this is appropriately a job for the Department of Commerce, rather than the USIA, the USIA has tripped badly in not priming the Commerce officials to take advantage of this showcase opportunity, and in not allocating funds for its costs, if necessary, from its now wasteful movie or canned news cable budgets.

Here is a field where the United States could easily have surpassed, which has been left irresponsibly to the Soviet sharpshooters.

To all the arguments which stress the need for a tighter, better coordinated and less costly program of American foreign information the partisans of USIA have one unvarying answer. We must get into the upper brackets in our information spendings, they say, because Russia is spending much more than we on foreign propaganda. President Eisenhower himself, in his American Legion speech in 1954, fell into this unfortunate error when he declared that for every dollar we spend on information, Russia spends fifty.

Despite the denseness of the Iron Curtain, we do know something about Russian propaganda expenditures. The often quoted figure of $1,500,000,000 a year for Russian propaganda waylays American spokesmen who are unaware that the figure includes the whole Russian annual outlay for newspaper, magazine and book publishing for domestic consumption. We have no way of disentangling the foreign propaganda figures from the gross total.

Americans who attribute a huge propaganda machine to Russia also overlook the glaring fact that practically all the pro-Communist publicity and indoctrination outside Russia are done not by the Russians themselves, but by the domestic members of the Communist Parties in the respective countries.

In European capitals, where USIA boasts sprawling and luxuriant establishments, and where regiments of USIA publicists are in conspicuous evidence, one searches in vain for corresponding Russian propaganda centers. Russia's propagandists work quietly and unobtrusively in the Russian Embassies or in the shabby headquarters of *Tass*. But when a really important setting presents itself for a Russian propaganda effort, as for instance at the recent Salonika Fair in Greece, Russia's showing is apt to be eye-opening in its magnitude, and in its exhibitional know-how.

Constant harping by USIA officials upon the comparative size of Russian propaganda is unfortunate because it diverts attention from the real Russian threat to our public information effort. That threat is qualitative, not quantitative. Russia outstrips our propaganda emissaries, not because she spends more money than we, but because Russian foreign policy is more salable to low-income groups in Europe, and colored racial groups in Asia, than is our own. Russia convinces, not by slick paper handouts, by high-brow books or by stupid documentary films, but by the tremendous argument of a sure-footed and winning foreign policy.

The most expert propagandists money could hire couldn't win respect or acceptance for Mr. Acheson's "wait until the dust settles" policy, or Mr. Dulles' Downing Street-haunted twists and turns. Only when our foreign information effort is synchronized with a dynamic and imagination-stirring American foreign policy can our foreign representatives hope to win the waverers of Europe and of Asia away from our Communist antagonists.

But perhaps the most disturbing indictment of prevailing USIA policies is that, all too often, they provoke Communist counter-propaganda. Frequently our highly touted USIA projects have the effect of stinging and goading Moscow into increased anti-American activity. The final result is that instead of silencing Red "hate" campaigns we provoke new difficulties for ourselves and magnify our problems.

In Washington, our top policy makers from President Eisenhower down are dedicated to the goal of a peaceful world. On occasion, they talk movingly about America's firm hope that ways may some day be found to live, without tension, in the same world with the Soviets. So far, so good.

However, the same top spokesmen in Washington who give voice to our country's peaceful aims and intentions, proclaim their intent to spend many more millions of dollars for enlarged and stepped-up anti-Communist propaganda campaigns overseas. These officials choose to ignore entirely our dismal propaganda failures of the past. Also, they fail to comprehend that one of the very great dangers of the foreign propaganda methods which we are presently pursuing is that these efforts needle the Soviets and cause them to intensify their abuse of the United States.

If we are to wage heated and continuous propaganda wars against the Soviet we must expect that Russia will wage retaliatory Cold Wars against us. Moreover, our unwarranted and wasteful propaganda to so-called neutral and friendly nations actually stimulates the

home-grown followers of the Moscow line to speak
against us. We furnish these Soviet followers with the
incentives to influence foreign people against our aims
and objectives and, still worse, our provocative type of
propaganda tends to make the man in the street throughout Europe believe that the United States and not the
Soviet Union has become the world aggressor.

Our Washington officials continually overlook the fact
that all other governments, except the Communists,
carefully refrain from this crisis-provoking kind of propaganda which our Government is resorting to with increasing frequency. Indeed, following our promotion
failures in Europe we are augmenting these extravagances in other parts of the world.

Perhaps the time will come when our Government
will realize that strong doses of overseas propaganda,
with still bigger doses advocated by men who should
know better, could very possibly provoke incidents. And
that's the explosive stuff that small—and large—wars
are made of! Thus, instead of spreading "truths" to all
mankind we are running the risk that our explosive
propaganda might one day kindle the fires that could
engulf all mankind.

A small example of this dangerous recklessness of our
propaganda planners was their announcement, made at
the crucial stage of the war in Indo-China, that American movie trucks had continually criss-crossed the firing
line. The USIA's press agent boasted, in his release to
the press associations, that our brave propaganda agents
were flirting with death in the furtherance of these pic-
ture-showing stunts. Fortunately no Americans were
killed in this reckless operation, but they might have

been. The USIA, in this instance, was willing to risk a shooting incident which might have involved us in actual war, simply to exhibit documentary films which were completely valueless as propaganda and especially so when shown to natives fighting for their lives.

Not content with these stupidities, the USIA announced in late 1953 that it was sending a camera expedition, headed by veteran ex-movie actor Cullen Landis, to roam for two years over Iran making "native life" and propaganda movies in that country. Iran happens to be one of the most explosive trouble-spots in the world today, located, as it is, just across the frontier from Soviet Russia.

The possibilities of a shooting incident, involving the innocents of the Landis expedition with its picture taking machinery and apparatus for movie showings to backward and excitable natives, are appallingly real. Total wars have been touched off in the past by no greater inciting situations.

The USIA is worse than useless to the American people as their voice abroad as long as this over-staffed and over-zealous Agency substitutes needling and crisis talk for sensible and effective informational efforts abroad. The present policy boils down to spending still more tens of millions of dollars in stepping up wasteful and harmful policies that result only in challenging the Soviets to competitive contests of ill-will and abuse.

17

More Give-aways Can Only
Give Us Grief

The pages of history tragically record that nations which condone red ink invariably end in the spilling of red blood.

Without fiscal balance there never can be real safety and security for Americans.

All that has been said about the superfluity of most of the functions of USIA could be said with equal force about its parallel and costlier contemporary, the Foreign Operations Administration.

Even the staunchest Congressional backers speak of FOA in terms of deep qualification. None has spoken more frankly than the highly respected Senator Walter F. George of Georgia. On July 1, 1953, Senator George rose to tell the Senate:

"As far as I am concerned, Mutual Security is going into its last fiscal year beginning this morning. The truth is that it ought to be terminated. . . . There is but one way for the nations of Western Europe to get, and stay, on their feet and that is to let them work their way out. . . . If after seven years of large appropriations from the Treasury of the United States, they are not now on their feet, they never will be."

But, despite the George admonition, Mutual Security, in the form of FOA, was back in the budget in 1954 and was granted another Treasury handout of $3,100,000,-000. In reality, the give-away program should have been terminated several years ago. It has been kept alive through the coalition of global-minded Democrats and Republicans who seem to believe that the giving away of dollars will cement friendship and who ignore the fact that dollars are never a substitute for leadership.

One of the silliest defenses of FOA was that made by a prominent Atlantic Seaboard Senator who declared that we must continue the FOA give-aways because America has a "moral" obligation to the nations who were the recipients. The Senator lost sight of the fact that these same nations, except in rare instances, feel no "moral" obligation to back the United States when their interests do not run parallel to ours. We saw unhappy examples of that when we sought their cooperation for a China coast embargo during the Korean war. The morality seems to be all on our side, the practicality on the side of our Allies. The day may come when we will find that we cannot eat our morality.

The most convincing reason why we should get out of the FOA was given inadvertently by President Eisenhower when he announced that we were in for a "forty-year" cold war. A short time later Director Streibert raised the forecast to fifty years.

If the President is right in this dismal prediction then we have a bear by the tail in FOA. If we must go on with this program for four decades, it will be the final straw that will break the back of our economy. And Russia, which is waiting ghoulishly and confidently for the crash of American economy, will have a clear path to world victory, according to her plans. It is the sound American economy which today, Atlas-like, is sustaining the free world. If our economy takes a tailspin we will see our Allies dropping away from us as leaves from a tree in autumn.

FOA's billions are a huge and hazardous charge on our economy. USIA's millions are a lesser charge but an equally dangerous one because through its ill-advised policies we risk the loss of the friendship and cooperation of the free world. America cannot further afford to support either of these two great extravagances—FOA or USIA.

The futile opposition of Senator George to the continuance of the give-away program was not the only voice raised in vain. Later in the year two able and influential members of President Eisenhower's Cabinet publicly proclaimed that the time has come to put the brakes on foreign aid and look to other methods of promoting world economic health and stability. Secretary of the Treasury George M. Humphrey said:

"The government must question both its right and its financial ability to continue to use the taxpayers' money to finance investments abroad on a large scale in the development of competitive enterprises." The Treasury Secretary added, "Our scale of taxation is already too high, and to maintain a sound and honest dollar we must bring our own expenditures and revenues into balance. We must continue," he said, "to examine most carefully every proposal to spend money whether it is a proposal for spending at home or abroad. The maintenance of our credit and of a sound dollar," the Treasury Secretary concluded, "is most important for foreign countries as well as it is for us here at home."

Secretary of Commerce Sinclair Weeks openly criticized what he termed "politics mixed with economics" and Mr. Weeks added the blunt warning that it was high time to halt "international handouts and global boondoggling."

One reason for the vitality of our hand-out policy is that its defenders skillfully conceal its viciousness under the cloak of misleading and high-sounding words. Thus, Washington never refers to the program as the rank subsidy which it is: in official language, it is always "aid to our Allies," or "defense," or "mutual security." Through some magic of words, the American people are persuaded that their billions are flowing away abroad to help America. The fact that the actual purpose of the handouts is to pay enforced tribute to unwilling "Allies," many of whom would unhesitatingly join the other side if we stopped subsidizing them, is obscured in the American mind. What any citizen would readily recognize in private life as a dishonorable shake-down is sublimated, in our foreign relations, into noble international Good Samaritanism.

If there were any sign, on the part of our deciding Washington leaders, that they are actually trying to discourage the outstretched palms, the weary American taxpayer could draw in his belt and wait hopefully for a better tomorrow. But there are no such signs. Instead, the subsidy stream seems to be widening and deepening.

Harold Stassen, in his frenzy to keep the billions moving, is now resorting to aerial globe-trotter trips to FOA-aided countries to prospect new ways of expending aid funds. Not long ago he flew to visit Tito in Jugoslavia: the day following Stassen's arrival Tito made him seem ridiculous by delivering a major public address declining to subscribe to the Lundon Bruto Agreement, declaring for co-existence with Red Russia, and condescendingly accepting Stassen's offered millions because the money was being ladled out without "conditions." Following this experience at the hands of Dictator Tito, who is again playing "cozy" with Moscow, Stassen hopefully flew to Spain, where he issued an announcement that Spain would receive $30 millions additional this year from Uncle Sam. Presumably, this handout to Franco will also be without "conditions."

The closing months of the year 1954 saw the welcoming red carpet stretched out almost continuously in Washington to receive distinguished foreign visitors. Each came to smile. To utter a few reassuring words. To get his cut of the tribute money. None went away empty-handed.

Prime Minister Mohammed Ali flew from Karachi to press the case for Pakistan. He went home with a pledge of $105,000,000.

President William V. S. Tubman of Liberia came next. He went home with the happy assurance that there would be a goodly sum for Liberia.

Third on the list was Chancellor Konrad Adenauer of

West Germany. The crafty Chancellor came to ask for a restoration of a mere half billion dollars of war-confiscated German property. In addition the Chancellor made it plain that he would be happy with nothing less than huge continuing American grants to underwrite the costs of West German rearmament!

Next, Britain's gracious Queen Mother "beamed" sweetly upon the Washington scene.

There followed the Prime Minister of Japan, Shigeru Yoshida. In his first public statement in New York, Mr. Yoshida stressed that he had come to the United States to thank the American people for past favors and great financial generosities accorded to Japan, and *not* "to ask for anything."

One week later, in Washington, D. C., Japan's chief diplomat changed his mind—and his tune! He boldly called for a revival of the Marshall Plan—this time for the Far East, to save the new countries of Asia from the sway of Communist China. Mr. Yoshida said, "Action less noble, less decisive than that will not be enough to tip the scales against communism." He added, "There is not much time, let us act now." Japan's former Prime Minister estimated the cost to the American taxpayer, for this proposed new give-away for Orientals, to be four billions of dollars annually. Moreover, this stupendous sum would be needed from now—until Eternity!

A second series of arrivals was to be Prime Minister Pierre Mendès-France of France, Julius Raab, Chancellor of Austria, Paul E. Magloire, President of Haiti, and the Prime Minister of Ceylon. Each would come hopefully to receive his share of the lush American handouts. None would be disappointed; all would be treated in the royal manner to which they are accustomed!

Without visiting Washington, two other countries have received rich slices of the American melon.

Iran, as a reward for replacing Mossadegh, was promised $30,000,000 on top of the $93,000,000 already handed over since the fall of "Mossie"!

Egypt, which has firmly rejected the presence of any American military mission in its country to supervise the spending of our give-away dollars, was promised $40,000,000 for the balance of 1954, with more to come.

Perhaps some of this money is not totally wasted in terms of American security. But it is deeply humiliating to the United States, at the crest of its power, that it must go out into the international market, checkbook in hand, to try to buy the allegiance of these political weak sisters. What staggers the American mind is the realization that, to keep them bought, the subsidies must go on almost indefinitely.

Unhappy confirmation of this fact appeared in the New York *Herald Tribune* of October 31, 1954:

"Harold E. Stassen, director of the Foreign Operations Administration, has proposed asking Capitol Hill to put the Mutual Security program and the staff that manages it on a permanent basis, since it is certain to be a 'permanent' policy undertaking for many years to come, regardless of political change."

Perhaps not enough of us are sufficiently aware that we are now facing that old domestic issue of "not enough money." Already the 83rd Congress has been forced to lift temporarily the National Debt limit to $281 billion, an increase of $6 billion. Meanwhile it is a little known fact that our 1955 deficit, of nearly $5 billion, almost parallels the handouts we are giving to foreigners in 1955!

This thought is worth repeating:

The United States will never be solvent unless we firmly resolve to eliminate activities and agencies of government which we can get along without or which we can greatly curtail.

On December 7, 1954, Senator Harry F. Byrd (Dem., Va.), long regarded as one of the nation's foremost authorities on fiscal matters, publicly proclaimed:

"I regard Secretary Humphrey as one of the ablest men who have ever guided the Treasury, but I am very much disappointed in his statement that there is no prospect of balancing the budget for the fiscal year beginning July 1, 1955.

"This means that we will then start the twenty-third deficit year in the past twenty-six. It is time that the Administration and the Congress face up to the reality of our fiscal situation. Since the deficit spending began we have increased the federal debt from $16 billion to approximately $280 billion.

"No prospect is now held out that the budget will be brought into balance this year or next. We are enjoying the greatest prosperity in our history. We are not engaged in war. If we cannot balance the budget now, I ask when can we balance it? Are we on a chronic deficit basis?

"During the period of this deficit spending we have accumulated astronomical debt. Our children and future generations must pay the interest, and some day they will have to pay the principal. Meanwhile, deficit spending has been the main factor in reducing the purchasing power of the American dollar from 100 cents in 1942 to 52 cents today.

"The foremost plank in President Eisenhower's campaign

was the promise of a balanced budget. A reduction of 7 per cent in government spending this year would place our financial affairs on a pay-as-you-go basis without increasing taxes. In the third year of his administration it is time that he fulfilled his campaign pledge.

"We have given away $40 billion to foreign nations, all of which has been added to the public debt. The first thing we should do is to eliminate economic aid to other countries, all of which have smaller debts than ours. Few will deny that there is opportunity for retrenchment by the elimination of waste and extravagance in every single activity of the government.

"If we continue to play Santa Claus to our people at home and half of the world abroad, we can expect nothing but collapse of our currency with all of its terrible consequences.

"The private enterprise system is based upon the principle that the people support the government and not the government the people."

In the case of the FOA, unless it is abolished, there will always be new crises and greater emergencies, either in Europe or elsewhere in the world, to justify its perpetuation and the maintenance of its unwieldy superstructure with its global payrolls. Likewise, in the case of the USIA new arguments and pleadings will always be plausibly offered for more and more millions to underwrite enlarged propaganda absurdities.

There is only one way to stop these superfluous programs. That way is by the elimination of both the FOA and the USIA. Whatever remaining functions the FOA may have can be carried out on a vastly reduced, carefully safeguarded and audited basis by the Department of State for economic activities and the Department of

Defense for military subsidies. The USIA, on the other hand, should be transformed into a compact, hard-hitting and honest news bureau of the Department of State.

When these sound steps are taken, Americans can hope once again to have a sound economy, without which there can be no permanent security or peace. We can look to one strong voice of America instead of two or more conflicting and harmful voices as at present.

18

Our Strength Is in Our Heritage

It is a melancholy thought to proud-spirited Americans that our prestige abroad is on a perpendicular down-grade. Foreigners, with some saving exceptions, don't like us. What is worse, they don't even respect us.

For this low estate we have only ourselves to blame.

A back-street *concierge* brought home this unpleasant truth to the author on a recent visit to Paris.

"You know, Mr. Castle, the Americans who come to France today aren't the same Americans whom we used to know in the Twenties," he informed me sadly.

"Those old Americans, with their big talk and their money to burn, used to annoy us, but we liked them. We used to think, what a grand country they come from.

"But the Americans today," and his voice took on a tone of regret, "they're not the same. These Americans come to live here. Most of them work for the American

Government. They trade in the PX. They live by themselves; we French people never get to know them well.
We wish they'd go home."

Some of our professional Europe pulse-takers would
do better to talk to more concierges and to fewer glad-
handers when they go to Paris. The wise old *concierge*
had happened onto a truth which explains many current political perplexities. Something has happened to
the magic which once invested the name "American"
throughout the globe. We are dangerously alone in a
world of envy and hostility. Our dollars have not been
enough.

The decline of American prestige overseas has gone
hand in hand with the decline of American patriotism
at home. We have lived into an era in which publicly
displayed patriotism has become something to be
ashamed of, outside the primary schools. In many circles it has become *passé* to be known as an undiluted
American. A new group, many of whom are well meaning, has arisen in our country to proclaim that old-fashioned Americanism is "primitive"—a smear word. Patriotism in their book is often adulterated with global
loyalties.

It was Herbert Hoover, the 80-year-old patriot, who,
speaking in Chicago, pointed out the social poison in
the current derision of American nationalism:

"We must realize," he said, "the vitality of the great
spiritual force which we call nationalism. The fuzzy-
minded intellectuals have sought to brand nationalism as
a sin against mankind. They seem to think that infamy is
attached to the word 'nationalist.' But that force cannot
be obscured by denunciation of it as greed or selfishness—

as it sometimes is. The spirit of nationalism springs from the deepest of human emotions. It rises from the yearning of men to be free of foreign domination, to govern themselves. It springs from a thousand rills of race, of history, of sacrifice and pride in national achievement."

It is perhaps too little realized that Americans who are ashamed of this noblest of political emotions rightly invite the contempt of foreign peoples.

The canker of diminished national pride cuts deep into our character as a people. It effects all of our contacts with other peoples, on either side of the Iron Curtain.

This new and ignoble American mood is reflected in the indifference with which so many Americans, in high official places, greet the most sacred national anniversaries.

The author has noted the hurt surprise with which he learned, in his travels through USIA-land, that the pretentious American information establishment in Egypt, where he happened to find himself on that day, was not even open on Washington's Birthday. Apparently the large USIA staff in this citadel of the Moslem world were playing golf or otherwise disporting themselves with private amusements. The Egyptian people were treated to the spectacle of a great nation which did not even stage a public ceremony to honor one of the most important of its patriotic days. Instead, its functionaries took a holiday.

But the reaction of these USIA subordinates is not surprising in view of the desuetude into which Independence Day has fallen, even in Washington, D. C.

It is interesting to note how the occupant of the most

difficult and most powerful office in the entire world—
the President of the United States—has spent the Fourth
of July on typical years of the last three administrations.
The author has looked them up. Here is what he found:

Eisenhower July 4, 1954	President Eisenhower rested with intimate friends at Camp David in Maryland.
Truman July 4, 1952	President Truman spent his last Fourth in office attending a baseball game.
Roosevelt July 4, 1944	On his last Fourth in office, President Roosevelt participated in no public ceremony, and no mention of his activities appears in the press.

In a nation where even the President has permitted
Independence Day to fall into disuse, it is not strange
that the common citizen becomes apathetic. What a
contrast with Communist Russia's May Day, when every high official of the State crowds himself upon the
reviewing platform to stand for hours at fixed attention
to honor the achievements of his country. It takes no
John Bunyan to point out to us that now, as always,
Faint Heart wins no victories.

In the great silence which surrounded the White
House on the Fourth of July in 1954, it was reassuring
that one voice rang out to remind the American people
of the responsibilities of their greatness. That voice was
that of Senator William F. Knowland. It was heart-
stirring to Americans who have grown accustomed to
mealy-mouthedness and double-talk from their statesmen to hear the Knowland pledge that he would resign

his Republican Senate leadership and begin to fight, if the United Nations staged another Communist appeasement. Such plain American talk was in an honored American tradition which is fast giving place to a national cringe.

The fact is not pleasant to contemplate, but the American people since 1945 have permitted themselves to be drugged by fears and hesitations and self-misgivings which have corroded the national will. We have been preoccupied, not by what we could do, but by what we couldn't do. We have erected bogeymen who have given us craven excuses for inaction. Our whole retreating policy since V-J Day which, with a few positive exceptions such as the Berlin airlift and the Inchon victory in Korea, has been a national blunder of the first magnitude. It has been inspired by forcible-feeble top statesmen who have written their own hesitations into a losing American foreign policy. Their one magic, at every critical juncture, has been to pour out American dollars to buy security with grant give-aways and worthless propaganda. It is a magic which hasn't worked.

USIA, FOA and all the other disillusioning American adventures in mass handouts have been only the inevitable reflection of a national leadership which shrinks from logical and direct decisions. If, as we have shown, the directors and the sub-directors whom we have hired to administer these billion-studded programs have been figures for ridicule rather than pride, the fault does not rest exclusively with them. It rests with the top statesmen who have given the FOA and USIA directors and their underlings ineffective and impossible programs to carry out.

The real indictment of the give-away programs must be directed against their conception, rather than their execution. Starting out with a false political premise—with a basically unsound approach to American foreign policy—the give-away programs, not surprisingly, have wobbled and careened to sick failure. Even administrators gifted with political genius couldn't have made them work. And the administrators whom we have chosen have not been geniuses.

There are stern limits to what an information operation can do for any nation. America's USIA and HICOG press agents, operating in such highly sophisticated countries as France, the United Kingdom, Germany, Italy, etc., countries which invented many of the propaganda techniques which we are now tardily discovering, only make America ridiculous when they try to sell myths to such people. When they solemnly lay down edicts of solvency and good financial housekeeping to Europeans, their listeners inevitably recall that America is the land of the perpetual deficit. When Europeans hear our fulminations against Communist Russia, they recall wryly that Russia is where she is today because the United States armed and equipped Russia through Lend Lease, opened the door of Asia to Russia through Yalta, and permitted the transfer of the atomic and hydrogen bomb secrets to Russia through its laxity in tolerating American atom spies. When they encounter our concern about Indo-China and an Asiatic Pact, they remember that it was an Acheson who rejected the idea of an Asiatic Pact in 1949 when Korea and the Philippines tried to sell it to the United States, and it was a Truman who fired General MacArthur when he was on the point of wiping out Chinese Communist aggressive power on the Asiatic continent.

Our inexpert Voice of America script writers and USIA cable letter authors cannot blink these historic facts when they adopt a preaching attitude toward Europeans and other members of USIA's captive audience. Most of them, faced by their hopeless task, merely go through the routine motions.

The answer to America's foreign information near failure lies, not in our confused alphabetic agencies, but in our national character. It is in the creeping enfeeblement which has been devitalizing the American national will. For this disastrous trend, the blame must attach to the irresolute, politically minded top statesmen who, in the post-war years, have led the American people down a great historic detour away from their true destiny.

Disheartening though our experiences in selling America have been, there is no warrant for despair. The quakings and the waverings are all in Washington; they are not in grass-roots America. The people's heart is sound. The transcendently great American economy is still the marvel of the world. Despite the advances of Communism, we and those who think as we do still bestride three-fourths of the globe. The power and the strategic advantage are in our hands, if we will have the self-certitude to use them.

America can be sold to the world as long as it is a strong America in which faltering, hesitating foreign peoples can find assurance and inspiration. It cannot be sold to the world if its leadership is "sicklied o'er with the pale cast of thought," and its policies molded in putty.

"There is nothing so powerful as truth," said Daniel Webster, "and often nothing so strange." The truth that America tells to the world in the years ahead will decide human history. It must be a truth which is in the tradition of the great American heritage.

Index